More Praise for *Know-How*

"As a learning and development manager, I make sure everyone else is successful in their work through learning. I often lean on occasional trainers to help me accomplish this huge task. *Know-How* offers guidance to help me reach this audience in an immediate and relevant way. I love how the authors emphasize that human connection is the heart of learning. I plan to use this book to empower our occasional trainers so they feel seen for the enormous value they provide."
—**Rula Andriessen**, Manager, Personnel Development, KHS&S Contractors

"Whether a manager, mentor, co-worker, or friend, we often find ourselves in positions where we have to pass our knowledge and skills onto others. Having the ability to do it right can be the difference between success and failure. *Know-How* will help you use your knowledge and expertise to help others in an engaging and effective way. Whether you're an occasional trainer or an expert, *Know-How* will give you the skills to put your know-how to use!"
—**Tim Slade**, Award-Winning Freelance E-Learning Designer

"*Know-How* delivers what it promises. Through vivid examples and dialogues about air conditioners, Apple watches, and corkscrews, Harold Stolovitch and Erica Keeps help occasional trainers discover how to translate their know-how into know-how-to."
—**Allison Rossett**, Professor Emerita, San Diego State University

"Stolovitch and Keeps never disappoint with the research-based guidance they provide in their writing. *Know-How* is chock full of steps, tips, and tricks on becoming a better occasional trainer. This is critical as we emphasize and embrace the practice of informal and social learning over more formal means of developing performance competence back on-the-job. Following it will also help improve the design and development of formal instruction!"
—**Guy W. Wallace**, Performance Analyst and Instructional Architect, EPPIC Inc.

"*Know-How* is a practical, accessible guide for parents, coaches, experts, and anyone who needs to effectively pass on what they know to others. The empathetic approach supports and centers learners, while the real-world _____ _____ ____ anyone tasked with training through tricky situatioı train our young son on how to use a bottle opener he was so proud of himself!"
—**Samantha Greenhill**, Communications Specialist

T0273545

"This fun, educational book is not just for those who find themselves cast into the role of informal, occasional trainer—it has a surprising amount of hard-hitting counsel and wisdom for those of us who have been training professionally for quite a while. Read this book if you want to discover how you can improve your training skills in any environment from a corporate compliance session to helping a friend or relative learn a new skill. The ideas, concepts, and advice will be effective no matter what content you have to convey."
—**Karl M. Kapp**, EdD, Professor, Instructional Technology,
   Bloomsburg University; Co-Author, *Play to Learn*

"This book is easy to follow and full of tips and effective techniques. I found it applicable not just when teaching my students but also for working with colleagues. Worth a read!"
—**Jennifer Rodriguez**, Third-Grade Teacher, Culver City, CA

"Many new hires at my small but expanding wholesale bakery possess very few English-language skills. Yet, we still have to onboard and train them in an unfamiliar environment on novel tasks, while maintaining safety, cleanliness, and quality standards. *Know-How* has already become a fantastic resource that I immediately put into action! It is easy to read, the examples are clear, and the application is fun and simple. I already see results. I recommend this book to anyone who must train but does not how to get started."
—**Rolf Bender**, Owner, Sunflour Bakery

"I love the easy, upbeat tone and confidence-building approach this book takes as it offers sound guidance to mentors, coaches, and trainers. It is a relatable guide to sharing one's own knowledge and empowering others to learn new things while supplying the tools needed for successful learning."
—**Trudy Blair**, Professional Dog Parent Trainer, Tully's Training

"If you've ever struggled to share what you know with someone, *Know-How* is the book for you! Read it, practice, and become a proficient occasional trainer. As a parent, teacher, and nonprofit volunteer, I've experienced first-hand how effective the techniques in *Know-How* are."
—**Petti Van Rekom**, EdD, Director, Civil Discourse, League of Women Voters
   of Orange Coast

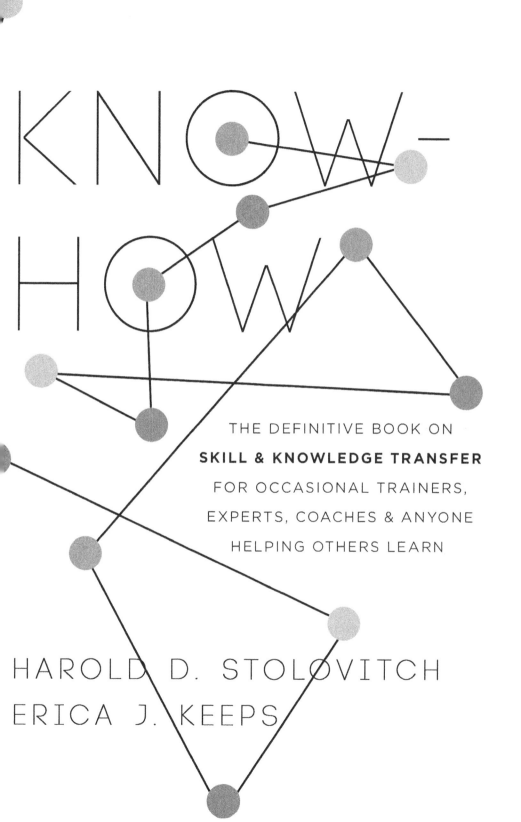

KNOW-HOW

THE DEFINITIVE BOOK ON
SKILL & KNOWLEDGE TRANSFER
FOR OCCASIONAL TRAINERS,
EXPERTS, COACHES & ANYONE
HELPING OTHERS LEARN

HAROLD D. STOLOVITCH
ERICA J. KEEPS

© 2021 ASTD DBA the Association for Talent Development (ATD) and Harold D. Stolovitch and Erica J. Keeps
All rights reserved. Printed in the United States of America.

24 23 22 21   1 2 3 4 5

No part of this publication may be reproduced, distributed, or transmitted in any form or by any means, including
photocopying, recording, information storage and retrieval systems, or other electronic or mechanical methods,
without the prior written permission of the publisher, except in the case of brief quotations embodied in critical
reviews and certain other noncommercial uses permitted by copyright law. For permission requests, please go to
copyright.com, or contact Copyright Clearance Center (CCC), 222 Rosewood Drive, Danvers, MA 01923 (telephone:
978.750.8400; fax: 978.646.8600).

Mah jongg tiles on page 115 are from tc397/DigitalVision Vectors via Getty Images.

ATD Press is an internationally renowned source of insightful and practical information on talent development,
training, and professional development.

ATD Press
1640 King Street
Alexandria, VA 22314 USA

Ordering information: Books published by ATD Press can be purchased by visiting ATD's website at td.org/books
or by calling 800.628.2783 or 703.683.8100.

Library of Congress Control Number: 2020942908

ISBN-10: 1-950496-27-9
ISBN-13: 978-1-950496-27-3
e-ISBN: 978-1-950496-28-0

ATD Press Editorial Staff
Director: Sarah Halgas
Manager: Melissa Jones
Community Manager, Learning & Development: Eliza Blanchard
Developmental Editor: Kathryn Stafford
Text Design: Michelle Jose
Cover Design: Molly Von Borstel, Faceout Studios

Printed by P.A. Hutchison Company, Mayfield, PA

To Buttercup—
Spending the last year transferring our know-how into your
know-how-to (and when-not-to) kept us constantly challenged. Much of
what we discovered when working with you was integrated into our discussions
and reflections for this book. Thank you! You have made this book so much
more meaningful to us and hopefully to our readers.
And thus, we gratefully dedicate this book to you.

Contents

Preface

Why have we written this book? We have spent more than half a century working with training, learning, and performance improvement professionals. Our research, energy, and efforts are focused on assisting our colleagues as they help people in the workplace learn things they need and value so that, in turn, they can achieve desired outcomes. Desired by whom? Most of all by themselves—they want to improve their impact. Their organizations and others, such as their managers, colleagues, customers, and the communities they serve, will also benefit from their accomplishments. We have also reached out to educators who are just as dedicated to helping children and adults achieve success in their studies. Nevertheless, we have always had the feeling that we were missing something . . . or perhaps it was *someone*. What about those who are facing the everyday challenges of helping people succeed and become independently capable? You know who we mean—the fellow worker, a confused child, strangers asking for directions, a friend struggling to use their new smartphone, a puzzled colleague trying to scan some documents, or even a new salesperson who's trying to develop a sales proposal.

We felt driven to transform what we have learned about training and learning into useful tools that anyone—not just training and learning professionals—can readily access and apply. This book is for them. It is based upon the sustained success and impact of our previous books, especially *Telling Ain't Training*, as well as feedback we have received throughout the years. A lot has changed during the last 20 years in the world of formal workplace training. There is so much more emphasis on the use of technology, learning management systems, and multimedia approaches to helping workers at every organizational level advance in their jobs. Interactive, web-based repertoires of courses and modules abound. A recent comprehensive survey from *Training* magazine about how the workplace delivers most of its training hours found that approximately 35 percent was delivered either fully or largely via live instruction.[1] About 25 percent of instructional hours were delivered online or through computer-based delivery systems. Almost 70 percent of training hours came to the learners in a blended fashion through various combinations of delivery modes. In addition, 10 percent of training hours were presented through virtual classrooms and webcasts, and about 2 percent of training hours reached learners and trainees through mobile delivery systems. This is typical of formal instruction in business, industry, the military, governmental agencies, health institutions, and many other workplace organizations.

Outside formal training spheres, a huge amount of informal training is taking place. The common ratio of informal (everyday interactions on the job in which some form of training or learning takes place) compared with formal training is quite surprising: 70-20-10. In this ratio, 70 percent of workplace training takes place as authentic job experiences and challenges, along with discussions, feedback, and interactions with individuals, which accounts for another 20 percent. That leaves 10 percent for formal training sessions delivered live, in blended form, or electronically. While this is not a scientifically derived set of percentages, it was formed through a consensus of professionals in the training field and observations of what goes on in the world of work.

Finally, in the social arena, outside the workplace, a large amount of one-on-one teaching and learning occurs every day: between parent and child, among friends and neighbors, by providing directions or showing someone how to play a new game or acquire a skill.

So much is written and said about the modern innovations that enhance training, improve efficiencies of learning, and save costs while inserting representations of the "real" world to display how things work. Learners get to see, hear, and even touch things in these virtual worlds. With this gain, however, may also come some loss. Teaching and learning principles have not varied much over time. Our environments may change with the arrival of virtual offices, technology advancements, continuous online communication, and social networking. However, when faced with an immediate need to become proficient at something, people typically prefer to have the reassuring comfort of a nearby helper. Do you need to thaw out a car door in deep winter, open a bottle of wine without a corkscrew, or interpret a hazardous materials label on a pallet you have to move? (How? With what? Where to?) There's nothing better than getting that generous offer of know-how so that you, too, can perform. A special joy of sharing occurs between the giver and the receiver when a transfer of know-how results in a person's success. No emoji or *bing!* sound quite replaces a human gesture or encouraging voice.

In this book, we have endeavored to produce a fun, effective guide for readers who frequently find themselves in the informal role of trainer, tutor, guide, coach, consultant, or helpful advisor. The book, simply speaking, is for people with any form of know-how that someone else requires—it's relevant for informal workplace learning and life in general. The writing cuts to the chase, providing what you need *now* to quickly get people learning and up to speed. No fumbling, bumbling, rambling, or messing with their heads.

Technology may be grand, but helpful, personal encouragement, along with an invitation to "call me if you need me," can be even better. Use all the resources you can find to build knowledge transfer. But never forget that the immediate, on-the-spot transfer of your know-how into another's know-how-to is incredibly effective if done right.

The tone of this book is light, personal, and direct, speaking to you conversationally as if we were together and chatting. The chapters are sequenced like stepping stones—each carrying you toward the goal of mastering occasional training. They provide brief explanations, guidance, tools, examples, and relatable, real-world applications. The start of each chapter presents a few bulleted highlights and ends with a short exercise prompting you to recall and apply what you have learned. To avoid too much telling, every chapter includes activities to engage you and reinforce your retention of key points.

The flow of the book is quite simple. The first chapter puts you right into the action and lets you know what the benefits are not only for those you help learn and perform but also for yourself. It includes lots of examples you can relate to and talks a bit about the book title. In chapter 2, you find out what an occasional trainer or OT is. An OT takes on an astonishing variety of roles, and you'll be surprised at how you can, and probably do, naturally assume them in your life. In chapter 3, we hit you with a big problem: We often get in the way of ourselves and others, even when we mean well and are working hard to explain how to. Fortunately, the chapter helps you recognize the traps and guides you out of them quickly. It also lays out the responsibilities of your learners.

Now you are ready to get into high action, and chapter 4 offers a sure-fire model and formula that raise the probability your training efforts will be successful. You get to apply the formula and receive feedback. The next three chapters build from this. Chapter 5 shows how to maximize learning by getting the learner to do most of the work. Chapter 6 brings in a whole new approach to *practice*, demonstrating how you can make it fun as you enhance learning, retention, and competent performance. Chapter 7 is one of our favorites. The title—"Tips, Tricks, Tools, and Tidbits"—says it all. Enjoy!

Chapters 8 and 9 focus on two key aspects of ensuring that what you do sticks to the person with whom you are working. Chapter 8 emphasizes the importance of fostering just the right amount of learner confidence. This is an important and recurring theme—how well you perform often depends on your level of confidence. Chapter 9 lays out a powerful rationale for providing learner support, even when you are no longer present. You already know that, when left alone after being trained, you still may feel somewhat uncertain. Creating personal support or providing helpful resources decreases these concerns. These chapters integrate the value of creating optimum confidence for the learner to exert the required effort and overcome inner doubts. With sufficient support, the learner is more likely to sustain that effort and succeed.

In chapter 10, you find out about the value of testing, especially in non-threatening ways. Testing is a great method to reassure your learners, and the chapter presents simple techniques and examples to practice. Chapter 11 focuses on you. It includes a self-assessment meant to reinforce what you have learned and sends you off with some final, useful advice.

The concluding chapter provides a repertoire of things you can and should do going forward. Apply these tips and techniques and you will achieve increasing successes and evolve into the most awesome trainer you have ever met.

After reading this book and applying the principles and practices, please share your experiences with us at hstolovitch@gmail.com or ekeeps@gmail.com. Your feedback is important!

How to Use This Book

This book is designed to ensure your learning experience is easy and fun. Its goal is to help you become an effective occasional trainer, strengthen your occasional trainer skills, and offer a different perspective on what your role can be. It starts out with the basics of what *know-how* is and why it is so important that you share yours effectively with others who need it. You'll get clear guidance on how to transfer your know-how to others, along with concrete, relatable examples and activities for you to engage in. The up-front highlights and end-of-chapter reviews reinforce key points and provide feedback on how you are doing. Use these to prepare for what is to come in each chapter and strengthen what is important to retain at its conclusion.

You'll find the following icons throughout the book:

Activity
Do the activity before you continue reading

Remember This
These exercises highlight key points to retain.

To gain the most benefit from the book, here are a few suggestions:

- Do all the practice exercises and self-assessments. The more you engage, the more you will learn and retain. Warning: The less you actively engage, the greater your danger of not being able to transform the book's words into actions!

- Set aside enough time to complete each chapter in a single sitting. It shouldn't take you longer than an hour—don't break the continuity. Plan ahead!

- Complete at least one chapter every week. If even a few days go by between chapters, revisit the Remember This review at the end of the previous chapter for a quick refresher to bring it all back.

- Whenever you encounter a scenario or activity, really get into it. Picture what is happening. Imagine that you are actively engaged in the situation.

- Visualization strongly enhances what you get out of what is written. Check out the photo of the two of us on the About the Authors page. Imagine that we're with you, sharing in the experience and chatting about what's going on.

- If you anticipate having to take breaks of more than a week between chapters, use a highlighter to call out important points. Write notes in the margin as you read. Then, whenever you return to the book, you can skim the pages to review your highlights and notes before heading into new territory. This helps to facilitate re-entry.

- Between chapters, try applying the principles and procedures you have just learned in real life. Find a peer or colleague who could benefit from some know-how you possess and use what you've learned to help them acquire it. Monitor how you did. Debrief your learner to discover how well you both performed.

- Read this book a second time. (It's not that long, we promise!) You may have missed some concepts the first time through that will jump out at you later. Or you may find that procedures that appeared awkward before seem easier to visualize and apply.

- Apply what you learn from this book as soon and as often as possible. The best way to hone your new skills is to seize opportunities to practice being an occasional trainer.

- Seek out opportunities to be a learner. Think about how you feel when you're being trained by someone else. Notice what works and what doesn't. Then apply that in your own training.

Acknowledgments

Undertaking the creation of any book demands a lot of thought, preparation, and discipline on the part of the authors. More than that, it requires the contributions and guidance of many people who possess expertise and experience in bringing a book to fruition. We were blessed with an ultra-capable ATD editorial and production team who continuously provided creative help and commentary throughout the organizing, planning, and execution of this volume. *Know-How* is small in stature but complicated in design, illustration, and tone in its attempt to address a variety of readers, from knowledgeable trainers to novices just starting out in the field.

Our most sincere thanks to Justin Brusino, who accepted to sponsor and support this unusual project for ATD. He took the risk of reaching out beyond the usual learning and development community to include anyone attempting to transfer what they know to another person. Broadening the reach to encompass such a large, almost endless audience took an act of faith. Thank you for your trust.

What can we say about Melissa Jones and her cheerful efforts to mold our manuscript into an engaging and credible book? Our thanks for her editorial guidance and creative crafting of all the book's components. We did not make life easy for her, yet she was always there smiling.

We offer much appreciation to the book's designer Michelle Jose and the rest of the book's ATD publication team, including Eliza Blanchard,

Kathryn Stafford, Sarah Halgas, Jamie Connelly, Kay Hechler, and Suzy Felchlin, who transformed our words and ideas into this attractive product and brought it across the finish line to market.

Special thanks to all of those, too numerous to mention, with whom we consulted and who read the book, tried out the exercises, and reported their experiences and impressions. You know who you are, and so do we.

To Patricia Rodriguez, you are our life support system! We appreciate every day how you look after and manage us so we can focus on our work. You make our lives a joyous, productive possibility.

And finally, our beautiful, playful, Havanese puppy, Buttercup, whom we adopted just as we were embarking on this book project. Both she and the book took over our lives for the next several months. Buttercup is full of energy, always demanding attention, but she also showers us with unconditional love and continuous challenges—many delightful, some not so much. We quickly discovered that all our research into transforming acquired skills and knowledge into performance was about to be put to the test. Like our pup, the manuscript required us to keep things simple and provide examples that were real, relevant, and relatable. We also found ourselves struggling to make our so-called teaching-learning expertise applicable to the doggie world as well as occasional trainer initiates.

As the book progressed, so did our knowledge of puppy (or, more accurately, pet parent) training, and we became immersed in an entirely new reality as we began working with super dog parent trainer Trudy Blair of Tully's Training. Trudy patiently coached us in our new roles—helping to form our knowledge and competence while building our confidence with Buttercup. Due to the pandemic, we began our lessons virtually via Zoom and FaceTime. Later, we met in parks—clad in masks and practicing social distancing—to drill Buttercup on commands with increasingly competing distractions. When our precious puppy graduated with honors and a diploma, we were the proudest parents! She had learned a lot and so had we. And this book is much better for it all.

Finally a word on the collaborative style of this publication. We are a husband and wife team who individually and together have dedicated our lives to helping people learn and perform in ways they and all those they affect value. We hold mutual professional and life goals. We appreciate what each of us brings to every project we undertake. We are delighted to seize this opportunity to exchange thanks to one another for the collaboration in producing *Know-How*. As always, in the process, we have learned a lot from each other.

If I Can Do It, So Can You

CHAPTER HIGHLIGHTS:
- What is know-how?
- We all possess a lot of know-how.
- Problem: How do I make my know-how yours?
- Examples and a set of rules.

Know-how. We all have it in one form or another. Know-how is simply practical knowledge or the skill and ability to do something. Do you have any of these know-hows? Check off all that apply.

- ☐ Assemble furniture
- ☐ Run a marathon
- ☐ Deactivate an alarm
- ☐ Program a setting on a device
- ☐ Play billiards
- ☐ Solve a Sudoku puzzle
- ☐ Unjam a photocopier
- ☐ _____
- ☐ _____
- ☐ _____
- ☐ _____
- ☐ _____

- ☐ Create a budget spreadsheet
- ☐ Dance a waltz
- ☐ Arrange a piece of music
- ☐ Bake a soufflé
- ☐ Complete a tax return
- ☐ Do a mail merge
- ☐ Play Yahtzee
- ☐ _____
- ☐ _____
- ☐ _____
- ☐ _____
- ☐ _____

Now use the extra spaces to jot down a few more know-hows you have that a friend, colleague, or kid might want to gain from you.

From Our Journal

While our own primary skills and knowledge are related to improving workplace learning and performance in ways valued by individuals and their organizations, we each have some interesting, personal know-hows. Harold is a marathon runner and mentor as well as an expert bed-maker. Erica knows how to bake healthy muffins, decorate homes, play Mah Jongg, and manage large-scale home- and work-related projects.

We all possess an almost endless list of know-hows that at some point someone might call on us to share. When that happens, how prepared will you be to meet the challenge of transforming your know-how into *their* ability to perform?

KEEP IT SHARP

Father: Son, why are there cuts all over your hands?

Son: I tried to slice some bread. The knife kept slipping, and I cut myself a few times.

Father: Well, it's probably because the knife is dull. Let me test it. . . . Yup. It desperately needs sharpening. Why don't you do it?

Son: I don't know how.

Father: You're always on your phone. Go to YouTube and find out.

Son: (Short time later.) Dad, I went online. It's frustrating. The first video clip showed me how to sharpen a knife with a whetstone. Do we even have one?

Father: No.

Son: The second one showed a person sharpening a knife when, suddenly, a piece of the blade flew off and nicked them in the face. You know how to do it. Can't you just teach me?

This brief scenario is a real one. The son discovers the knife is dull and asks for dad's help. He sends his son to YouTube for assistance. But it didn't work. So the son turns back to his dad to acquire his knife-sharpening know-how.

While this example might appear simplistic, it is nevertheless common for people to feel helpless when faced with tasks they are not equipped to handle. And, if that task offers little challenge for you to masterfully execute, it should be a no-brainer for you to simply "show them how." Sure, it's intuitively obvious, but our research has consistently demonstrated that what appears to be simple—whether it's a local resident providing directions to an out-of-town visitor or a fellow worker helping to safely lift a heavy object—often goes awry. Stuff happens. Simple becomes confusing. Both giver and receiver end up frustrated: If I know so much, why can't I make people learn?

Let's begin with a few success stories and then figure out what went right. Read each scenario and observe closely to determine what happened.

MOVING RIGHT ALONG

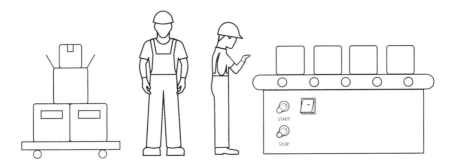

New Hire: I've tried to turn on the conveyor belt three times. But it just won't start. I can't figure it out. I checked to make sure the power is on. Why can't I get it going? [*Frustration. Feeling stupid.*]

You: What exactly do you want to do?

New Hire: Place all the items in this cart onto the conveyor and send them along to sorting and packing. But when I press the START button here, nothing happens.

You: Got it. So, if you can get the conveyor belt started, place the items on it, make sure that the items are moving smoothly and en route to the next point, you'll feel good?

New Hire: Yeah!!

You: OK. Take a close look at the START button. What do you notice just to its right?

New Hire: Hmmm. Now that you mention it, it looks like a blue switch.

You: Good eye. Any idea what it's for? Think.

New Hire: Does it have anything to do with the START button?

You: Let's find out. Press down on the blue switch with your right hand and while still pushing, press the START button with your left.

New Hire: Wow, it started up! [Excited.] I guess that this blue switch acts as a safety measure by making sure you're clear when the conveyor starts. Both of my hands had to be clear of the conveyor to press the buttons. Clever!

You: You've got it! Now, hit the STOP button. Great! Notice that there's no safety switch. Why not? Think.

New Hire: Hmmm. Maybe because if you have to stop quickly, you shouldn't waste time with another switch.

You: Right! OK. Now, start the conveyor again when it's all clear and ready. You should never start if anything is on the belt. Do you know why?

New Hire   So that things don't fall off when the belt starts to move?

You: Right, again!! It can be a bit jerky when the belt begins to move. Always start clean and clear. Nothing on. No obstructions.

New Hire: Got it.

You: OK, then . . . start her up. Tell me what you are going to do, then do it. Once it's going, load the items on one at a time. Continue to load as they move through. Stop if anything falls over or off the conveyor or if there's a jam. Go!

New Hire: [A bit nervous.] OK. Press down the blue switch and hold it there. Press START at the same time with left hand. Once it's moving, place items on the conveyor one at a time. Watch for wobbles or falls of any kind. Keep an eye open for jams. OK, the last one is through the hatch, so . . . STOP. Thanks, man! [Relieved and jubilant.]

You: You did great! Happy to help. Good luck on the job. Keep on using your head. Call on me if you run into any trouble. My call number is #445. Never hesitate to ask for help. [Smiling.]

New Hire: I sure will! [Smiling and feeling good about his accomplishments. Ready for the next challenge.]

 PRACTICAL
EXERCISE

Now, let's review what happened. Check off each item you noticed that took place.

The New Hire expressed need.
- ❏ You asked what the New Hire wished to accomplish.
- ❏ The New Hire stated desired outcome.
- ❏ You restated desired outcome in specific terms and sought confirmation.
- ❏ You engaged the New Hire's attention with leading questions.
- ❏ You guided the New Hire to infer next steps and encouraged thinking and acting.
- ❏ You congratulated the New Hire for successful accomplishment of desired outcomes.
- ❏ You released the New Hire and offered follow-up support.

Who did most of the work?
- ❏ You (the trainer)   ❏ New Hire

The New Hire:
- Expressed the need and desired accomplishment.
- Located the blue switch and correctly inferred its purpose.
- Started the conveyor and stopped it.
- Loaded the conveyor and monitored the progress of all items.
- Shut down the conveyor.

While you:
- Confirmed what success would look like.
- Asked leading or guiding questions and recommended actions.
- Reinforced and congratulated the New Hire's success and offered follow-up support.

Through your guidance, the learner did most of the work, achieved the goal, and is now the proud owner of a piece of your know-how. Bravo!

The next scenario tells a more complicated story. You may not get all the details, but you can still read it through and note the similarity of training style. At the end of the training scenario, we'll review what took place, focusing on how the transfer of know-how progressed.

A DIFFERENT PICTURE

Sales Leader: Jerry suggested you could help me develop a set of PowerPoint slides for a group of salespeople. He gave me a set of his old slides to use as a base and told me to change slides to replace old content with new stuff.

You: Show me what you have and explain exactly what you want to accomplish.

Sales Leader: Here's one of Jerry's slides:

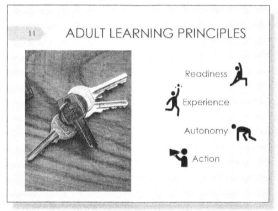

I want to change the left panel title, change the right panel words, and reuse the design and graphics.

You: Let's be clear. You want to produce a new slide that looks like Jerry's current one, but has your words and the same graphics correctly lined up.

Sales Leader: Exactly!

You: Great! Let's get started. You do the work. Notice all the small images to the left. Scroll down to Jerry's slide 11 and click once on it.

Sales Leader:

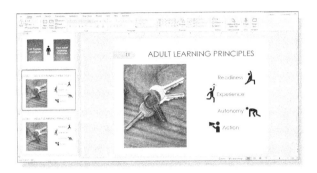

OK. When I place my cursor on the small image that's numbered 11 on the left and click once an orange box appears around it.

You:

Yes!! Now place your cursor on the slide with the orange outline and right click. Look at the menu that appears. Since you want to work on a copy of the slide, what should you do?

Sales Leader:

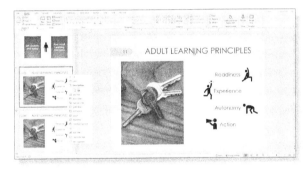

[Puzzled for a moment, then with a bit of hesitation . . .] Select and click on "Duplicate Slide"?

You:

Great call! Do it. Notice what has happened. You appear to be on the same slide, but now it's slide 12. Now, move to the bigger slide image on the right. At the top of the slide, it says, "Adult Learning Principles." Click on that title. What do you see around the title you just clicked on?

Sales Leader:

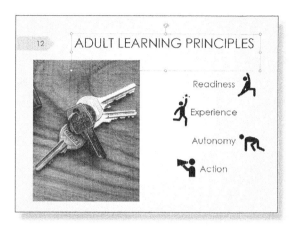

White dots.

You: Yes. Now place your cursor after the word principles and continuously press backspace on your keyboard until you've erased all three words. What do you do next?

Sales Leader:

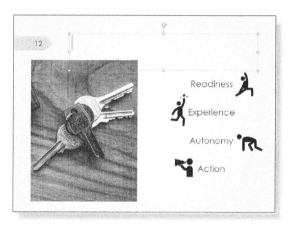

I guess I type in my new title. And I want it in title caps.

Sales Leader:

You: Go for it. Excellent! Now switch to the panel on the right and . . .

Sales Leader: I know! I click on any word, backspace to erase, and type in my word. [Excited.]

You: Sounds like you're on a winning streak. [Smiling and offering a pat on the back.] You go ahead. I'll monitor. Start with "Readiness" and then. . . .

Sales Leader: [Taking charge.] I know. Erase, type, then proceed onward one at a time. Voila! All done. This is great! [Proud and grinning.] The only problem is that some of the graphics are now covering text. How do I clean this up?

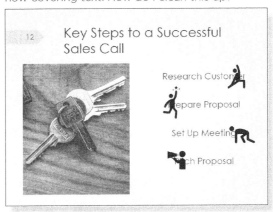

You: Hey, no worries! Click on the top graphic. What do you notice?

Sales Leader: A dotted box around it.

You: Now click inside the box and as you do, move your cursor. What happens?

Sales Leader: The graphic moves around.

You: Exactly! Now, move it until you're happy with the placement. Then click on the next graphic and move it into the right place.

Sales Leader: So, I do this for each one?

You: Yes. Now try this. When you select the last graphic for "pitch proposal" move your cursor to the top of the screen and look for the selection pane toward the right. Once there, click on the small triangle image with the circular blue arrow and select "flip horizontal" from the menu. Watch what happens.

Sales Leader: The bugle graphic flipped to face right.

You: What next?

Sales Leader: I need to move the graphic to face "pitch proposal."

You: Save, and you're done!

Sales Leader: Fantastic, and I did it myself! [Feeling proud]

You: Right. Now repeat this procedure for each slide you want to change and delete the slides you don't want to keep. The slides will automatically renumber themselves in the proper sequence. I also suggest making a copy of Jerry's original slide set in case you have any problems. Holding on to the old slide set is a good safety measure.

Sales Leader: I can't thank you enough. I feel confident that I can proceed on my own. But what if I run into trouble? [Somewhat nervous.]

You: Text me at this number for help or more tips, and I'll get right back to you! And . . . well done. I'm glad you figured most of it out for yourself. You're a champ!

 PRACTICAL EXERCISE

Scenario 2 is considerably more complex than the first scenario, and it required many more steps to achieve the desired goal. Nevertheless, if we apply the same checklist as before, we can verify whether the same things occurred.

❑ The Sales Leader expressed need.

❑ You asked what the Sales Leader wished to accomplish.

❑ The Sales Leader stated desired outcome.

❑ You restated desired outcome in specific terms and sought confirmation.

❑ You engaged the Sales Leader's attention with leading questions.

❑ You guided the Sales Leader to infer next steps and encouraged thinking or acting.

❑ You congratulated the Sales Leader for the successful accomplishment of desired outcomes.

❑ You released the Sales Leader and offered follow-up support.

Once again, who did most of the work?
❑ You (the trainer)
❑ Sales Leader

Sales Leader:
- Expressed the need and desired accomplishment.
- Identified what needed to be done and executed each step.
- Took charge of the tasks to be accomplished, even anticipating some.
- Made decisions and tried out new actions.
- Met the desired goal.

While you:
- Confirmed what success would look like.
- Asked leading or guiding questions and recommended actions.
- Reinforced and congratulated the Sales Leader's success.
- Extended follow-up support.

Notice that in both scenarios, the pattern was the same:
- drawing out the need
- clarifying the valued outcome
- guiding through questions to elicit successful learner responses and actions
- providing opportunities for productive practice with feedback and continuous reinforcement accompanied by encouragement
- letting the learner know support is available after the training session is over.

You can help people learn in a variety of situations—a fellow worker stocking shelves, a cocktail server organizing and balancing drinks on a tray, a bewildered visitor needing clear directions to the museum, or even your grandchild baking a cherry pie as delicious as yours. All it takes is what you witnessed in the two scenarios. It is not that difficult to transform your know-how into know-how-to for others. It just requires some tools and techniques that you can learn and practice to make it work.

Know-How for All

There is no greater thrill than the sense of accomplishment that comes with being able to shout, "Yes, I can do it!" Pride of achievement and great feelings of self-worth. Sadly, the reverse is also true. The dejection that comes from not being able to do it, even after someone has earnestly tried to explain, perhaps for the third time, can be terrible. There's often a horrible self-judgment of "something's wrong with me." This same sense of defeat also drains the energy from you—despite earnestly giving your all, you find yourself asking, "Why couldn't I get my charge to succeed?"

The benefits of successfully sharing know-how are numerous: the ability to perform or succeed at something valued, the joy of helping someone take flight, independence, productivity, time and effort savings, goal accomplishment, a sense of self-esteem, and so much more. While the book is called *Know-How*, we could have called it *From My Know-How to Your Know-How-To*. That's what this book is about—making your know-how someone else's. All it takes is a clear focus on the result, a productive questioning technique, and letting the learner do the heavy lifting. More on this in the next chapter.

 REMEMBER
THIS

Here's a brief exercise to help you remember a few key points from this chapter. Select the word or phrase option in parentheses that best fits each of the following statements.

1. Know-how is (*knowing what things are/practical knowledge or the ability to do something*).
2. (*Very few possess/Almost everyone possesses*) a broad range of know-how in one form or another.
3. Being able to use a knife sharpener to sharpen a knife that can slice bread easily (*qualifies/does not qualify*) as know-how.
4. The ability to make your know-how someone else's (*is easy and based on commonsense/is often problematic and confusing*).

5. Whenever possible, you should release the learner (*with a means for obtaining later support/with good wishes for independent success*).

6. When providing your know-how to another (*express and confirm specifically/let them imagine*) what success will look like.

7. The person you help acquire the ability to do something (*can and should/can never and should not*) own the new know-how.

8. The benefits of sharing know-how are (*all for the learner/for you and the learner*).

Now that you have made your choices, let's look at ours, along with our rationale.

1. Know-how is *practical knowledge or the ability to do something.* Knowing what something is is straightforward knowledge. Know-how implies being able to perform in some way. "How" is the key word.

2. *Almost everyone possesses* a broad range of know-how in one form or another. Know-how helps us survive. Even the ability to bring food to your mouth is a form of practical knowledge. (Observe any baby learning to eat.) Everyone has lots of it.

3. Being able to use a knife sharpener to sharpen a knife that can slice bread easily *qualifies* as know-how.

4. The ability to make your know-how someone else's *is often problematic and confusing.* Have you ever asked a local to give you directions when visiting a new town? Are you nervous and confused even when that person categorically assures you that "it's really quite easy" or confidently states, "Well, there are a few ways to get there." Knowing how to do something or get somewhere is a far cry from being able to transfer that know-how to a novice. (Sure, it's easy or there are a few ways to get there—for you.) Any experienced teacher or trainer knows how difficult the process can be. Incidentally, drop the idea of "commonsense"—it is subjective. Never trust it. Research methodology cautions that commonsense is the greatest enemy of science.

5. Whenever possible, you should release the learner *with a means for obtaining later support.* While good wishes are charming, it is far more helpful to reassure the learner that help is at hand if they run into difficulties. Even what appears to be the simplest task may require follow-up help if they need to recall a step, execute an action properly, or remember a detail. Extend a lifeline and provide a job aid, resource, or phone number to help maintain and strengthen know-how. We'll cover more on this in chapter 9.

6. When providing your know-how to another, *express and confirm specifically* what success will look like. The clearer the end-result— meaningfully communicated to and understood by the learner— the more easily they will "get it." Eliminate ambiguity and vagueness.

7. The person you help acquire the ability to do something *can and should* own the newly acquired know-how. That is what this book is all about. Instill ownership of the know-how in your learner. It should be shared readily and freely. If you are possessive of your capabilities, do not become a trainer, coach, advisor, or helpful colleague, parent, or friend!

8. The benefits of sharing know-how are *for you and the learner.* The more efficiently and effectively you get the learner to perform well, the greater the satisfaction of accomplishment for both of you.

Ready to move on? You have taken the first giant step into what is an important and possibly a new role for you—that of an occasional trainer. So, what exactly does this mean? Read on to find out!

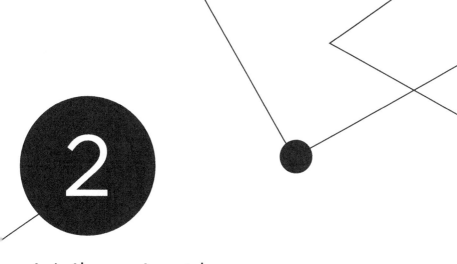

2

Who Is the "Occasional Trainer?"

CHAPTER HIGHLIGHTS:
- Where do occasional trainers come from?
- Do you have to know you are an occasional trainer to be one?
- Occasional trainer: assignment or accident?
- The occasional trainer challenge: Emphasize your own know-how or others acquiring know-how-to from you.
- Anyone can be an occasional trainer (OT).

An OT is someone who, from time to time, finds themselves in the role of teacher or trainer. It is not their full-time occupation. Sometimes, they don't even realize they have become a trainer, teacher, coach, or guide. Is this  you? Often, because of your work or life experience, practice, or trial and error, someone will reach out to you deliberately, spontaneously, or accidentally for help. They recognize your know-how—your competence—even though you may not feel up to their expectations. So, it is only natural to recruit you to assist someone who wants or needs to acquire some of the competency repertoire you own. The "occasional" part of the term in OT means that you, in the teaching, learning, coaching role, are only called upon to do it from time to time. You may never have thought about occupying this position, but there you are.

Pause for a moment to reflect on the last time you were thrust into a teaching or training situation.

But don't think of that time when someone said, "Can you do this for me?" Concentrate on a time when someone more emphatically said, "Can you teach me, show me, or help me learn to do this?" Were you pressed into the role formally (voluntold)?

Do any of these sound familiar?

- "Hey, we just brought in a bunch of new people to temp for the holidays. They need to know how to [*fill in the blank with random tasks*]. You're good at that. Get them up to speed during the next few days. They just need to be able to fill in. They'll learn as they go."
- "You're the best person we have available on [*insert company-specific system*]. A few members of the team don't quite get how the system works. For the next few weeks, I'd like you to make sure they become system savvy. You're a whiz at this—if anyone can do it, you can. I'll rearrange your work schedule a bit."

- "Josephine quit, so we're assigning Carl, one of our daytime front desk hotel clerks, to take over on your nights off. For the next week, train him to do the relief night auditor work she did. You broke in Josephine a few years ago. I'm sure you can do the same for Carl."

Or was it more accidental—even spontaneous?

- "I can't figure out how to calibrate this electronic lathe. I've never used one like this, and it looks complicated. You seem like an expert; can you show me how to turn fancy bowls and spindles like you? Can you help me make the right adjustments to vary my designs more while improving accuracy? I'm really excited and nervous about what this machine can do!"
- "Dad, you know how airbrushes work. I want to paint my mega action figures! Can you show me how?"
- "Do I really have to debone these chickens? I looked it up online, and it seems really complicated. You do it all the time. Can you get me started and give me some tips as I progress?"

In each case, you possess the know-how. However, as an OT (by assignment or request), your job has changed. You have to transform your know-how into another person's know-how-to—so they get up to speed, become system savvy, take over a job, calibrate a lathe, airbrush mega action figures, or debone chickens. Your challenge is not whether you have the ability to perform tasks, but if you can get others to be able to do them.

From Our Journal

Years ago, the Canadian Railway System undertook a major regulations overhaul regarding how railways were run throughout the country. And to make it more complicated, until the new regulations came into effect at midnight on December 18, everything would continue operating under the old regulations.

The changes would affect every aspect of operating the trains and touch every railway worker—from those who maintain the tracks, to signals specialists, to those running the trains, to the dispatchers and everyone handling freight—and even passengers. They were also dramatic. Any error could have huge consequences—equipment and infrastructure damage, work slowdown or injuries, accidents and fatalities, and collisions, fires, explosions, spillages, and derailments to name just a few.

We were consulting and developing training for one railway to help them make the switch. We had 20 months to do all the analysis, design, and development work, and help train the company's 42,000 workers be ready to change their status quo. We also had to prepare to evaluate once the changeover began!

Because everyone was forbidden to apply their new knowledge in their daily work until changeover happened, we determined that three months was the optimal timeframe to prepare all workers on the new regulations. Start before three months and the workers would forget the new information. Start closer to "show time" and there would not be enough time to train everyone.

How would our team of 12 professional regulations trainers accomplish this task?

We selected high-performing workers from each job category and made their training assignment a special high-profile appointment—Occasional Regulations Trainers (ORT). These 100 workers had been selected because of their excellent performance on the job and their quick-wittedness in dealing with change. They were removed from their regular jobs and given intensive training on the changes, well-designed materials, lots of practice and feedback from the regular professional trainers, and a rigorous training schedule to prepare everyone for the upcoming change. In these sessions, the ORTs were building up a store of know-how on the new regulations.

When they were ready to begin training the rest of the company, the ORTs began to show up on shifts to rehearse and practice with the workers, and refresh their new knowledge with simulation sessions. In addition, every worker trained by the ORTs had to pass rigorous tests. They trained continuously and intensively and always with the warning: DO NOT USE UNTIL midnight December 18!

As the deadline approached, the ORTs transformed into on-the-job experts and coaches. On December 19 they began riding the trains, assisting work crews and dispatchers, supervising depots and stations, and monitoring all operations as they provided feedback on application of the new regulations. And they continued doing this for the next six weeks to verify performance.

A rigorous audit of the conversion from operating under the old regulations compared with the new ones found that the effort had resulted in far fewer incidents and accidents than anticipated. In fact, the railway actually experienced a decline in incidents and accidents.

Once the transition was over, the ORTs returned to their previous positions but kept their new responsibilities of monitoring operations and sharing their acquired expertise within the work environment. All in all, this was a remarkably successful training venture thanks to the use of occasional trainers!

No matter how you assume the mantle of OT—whether it was thrust upon you, you evolved toward it, or you got sucked into it—you should be ready and able to wear it capably.  Welcome the opportunity when it arrives! Once you master the skills of the OT, you will not only better understand your own know-how, but you will also stand out for whom and what you are. As your know-how transfer skills grow, you will find numerous opportunities to apply them elsewhere, making others' lives easier as you create independence. Armed with what follows in the next chapters, you will become increasingly able to perform beautifully and with mounting success.

 ## A Transfer Activity for You

Here is a challenge activity for you to put into practice what you have learned. Select a know-how you possess. If you're having trouble coming up with one, use this list to stimulate your thinking:

- Play a simple game (Parcheesi, Checkers, Black Jack).

- Prepare a food item (bake cookies, prepare a tuna melt, make a pizza, fry an omelet).
- Maintain your car (check, add, or change engine oil; check and adjust tire air pressure; change windshield wipers).
- Adjust settings on a photocopier (change the paper tray, paper size, or turn on duplex printing) or operate the copier.
- Use different smartphone features (change WiFi network settings, create a hot spot, do creative photography).
- Perform tasks in the workplace (make a sales transaction, credit a refund, operate a tow-truck winch, modify a software application, reconfigure a spreadsheet).

Now, find someone who could use that know-how. Act as an OT and transfer that know-how to the learner until they can demonstrate that they can do it too.

After you've finished, ask yourself if:

❑ You and the learner stated the desired outcome in specific terms upfront.

❑ You guided the learner's attention using leading questions.

❑ You helped the learner infer next steps and encouraged thinking and acting.

❑ You congratulated the learner for achieving their desired outcomes.

❑ You released the learner and provided follow-up support.

What changes would you would make on future attempts? Debrief with your learner. And then congratulate yourself on your heroic effort!

 REMEMBER THIS

As you did in chapter 1, read each statement below. Select the italicized option within the parentheses that you think is correct. Then, compare your choices with ours and examine our comments.

1. Occasional trainers are (*tremendously varied/relatively similar*) in their backgrounds, experiences, and characteristics, and pop up in (*clearly defined work and life situations/ all walks of life*).

2. An OT is (*a formally recognized job classification/anyone who trains while mostly doing other things*).

3. What sets you up to become an OT is (*your know-how that someone else needs to acquire/your position as an exemplary model to learn from*).

4. What makes you a great OT is the strength of your (*know-how/ ability to transfer your know-how into others' abilities to perform*).

Now let's compare your choices with ours. We include comments for our selections.

1. Occasional trainers are *tremendously varied* in their backgrounds, experiences, and characteristics, and pop up in *all walks of life*. From juggler to pizza maker to gardener to artificial intelligence specialist, everyone has valuable know-how. Anyone can be drafted into or assigned the OT role.

2. An OT is *anyone who trains while mostly doing other things*. OTs do a lot of other stuff besides training. Hence, the "occasional" trainer.

3. What sets you up to become an OT is *your know-how that someone else needs to acquire*.

4. What makes you a great OT is the strength of your *ability to transfer your know-how into others' abilities to perform*. That's what great OTs do!

Turn the page to the next chapter to find out how to achieve this.

3

Step Aside: How I Trip Over My Expertise

CHAPTER HIGHLIGHTS:

- What is a SME and are you one?
- The giant distinction between being able to do something and being able to explain how you do it.
- The blunders we make when we try to explain.
- Easy ways to avoid the blunders.
- The role and responsibilities of the learner (the one you are helping acquire your know-how).

What Is a SME?

A subject matter expert (SME) is someone who has mastered an area of expertise. This is a fuzzy but extremely important term. Some use it to describe highly qualified, recognized experts, but we have a different take on it. You don't have to be the grand master of a specific subject or possess extraordinary work capability to qualify as a SME. So long as you know more than those looking to learn from you, that makes you the SME.

Let's think about this in real life. Imagine that I am lost in a big building and desperately need to find the restroom. You work in the building, have used the restroom many times, and know exactly where it is. Congratulations! You're a SME—a subject matter expert in getting to the closest washroom. Since you possess the requisite capability to "get the job done" in an expert fashion, we say this qualifies you as the SME. Anyone who has the skills and knowledge to accomplish what the learner requires magically becomes a SME!

Let's go into a bit more detail. We've already stated that knowing how to do something (or possessing know-how) does not mean that you then can effectively communicate your knowledge and capability to another person. Being able to do something and being able to explain, demonstrate, show, or guide how to perform the task are two very different things. Research on expertise has produced two clear conclusions:

- Knowing how to perform does not mean knowing how to explain how you perform.
- The greater your expertise, the greater the distance between you and novice learners.[2]

The two characteristics of expertise cited here are related to the nature of the subject: Expertise is the ability to perform in unique and extraordinary ways but not necessarily explain how it is done. Experts and novices in a given area think and process information about the subject matter differently. The greater the expertise, the greater the gap between expert and novice.

Bottom line: You can get to the restroom with no problem in lickety-split time. Can you help me get there on my own, please, before it's too late?

Let's move on to concrete instances in daily work and life situations.

DIAGNOSIS AND REPAIR OF A NOISY AIR CONDITIONING UNIT

Brother-in-Law: (On the phone, worried.) Harry, my air conditioner is chugging away and making horrible noises. I'm afraid it's going to die. You're the Mr. Fix-It in the family. Help me!

Harry: Did you turn off the A/C?

Brother-in-Law: Yes.

Harry: Good start! You are going to have to troubleshoot it. If I understand correctly, you want to stop all the bad sounds and get it working properly again, right?

Brother-in-Law: Yeah, I want it blowing quietly without strange sounds. . . . Your sister is really upset. But you want me to troubleshoot? I don't know how to do anything mechanical!

Harry: By the end of this call, you'll have acquired a new capability. (Smiling) My sister will be proud of you. Now, go look underneath the A/C unit in the small closet upstairs. Yours is just like mine. You should see a cardboard frame, roughly two feet wide, slipped into the bottom of the unit. There's a stretched, soft filter cloth held inside the frame. Go look now but stay on the line with me.

Brother-in-Law: Yeah, I see it. But the cardboard frame is filled with about an inch-and-a-half-thick layer of dirty, soggy dust fuzz. I don't see a soft cloth anywhere.

Harry: OK, you're looking at the air conditioning filter. It's just clogged with dust and dirt, which is choking the air conditioner intake. When did you last change that filter?

Brother-in-Law: . . . . I didn't know there was one.

Harry: OK. Spread some newspapers in front of the unit and slowly slide out the dirty filter. Be careful and don't breathe in the stuff.

Brother-in-Law: It's out. Yuck! OK, what now? Should I use a rag to clean around where the filter was?

Harry:	Good idea! Do you see a box labeled air filters beside the A/C unit? I put it there as a house-warming gift when you moved in.
Brother-in-law:	Yeah. I never noticed that before. Should I pull one out and slide it in where the old one was after I wipe around?
Harry:	(Smiling) Now who's thinking like a Mr. Fix-It? Do that and then wrap the old filter in the newspapers to get rid of it.
Brother-in-law:	(A few moments later) All done. That was really easy! (Sounding self-assured)
Harry:	Great! Now turn the A/C back on. Hear any weird sounds? Could you do this by yourself in three months? Make a note!
Brother-in-law:	Wow! Blowing quietly and smoothly. I fixed it. Me! So, I need to change the filter every three months? Duly noted! And, of course, I can now do it myself.
Harry:	Hey, man. You're a champ; I'm proud of you. Call if you run into any more problems. And say hi to my sis for me.

What this case clearly illustrates is that Harry, the possessor of the air-conditioning know-how, set his brother-in-law at ease, listened to and verified the need, and then, in easily understood terms, guided his brother-in-law through simple, carefully sequenced activities that allowed him to practice, verify results, and obtain feedback. Harry (acting as the SME) was able to transform his know-how into his brother-in-law's know-how-to. He met the two essential criteria of an OT:

- able to perform
- able to explain and guide the novice to perform successfully

He also verified performance success, congratulated the learner on his accomplishment, and provided an opportunity for follow-up assistance if required.

The same pattern could be applied to any setting and for almost any SME. For example:

- **Sales:** A highly successful salesperson could help an inexperienced one learn how to close a sale.

- **Sports:** A professional hockey player could show young amateurs how to protect themselves from the effects of a fierce body check.
- **Music:** A seasoned musician could encourage a young, technically capable instrumentalist to bring out widely divergent moods from a single piece of music.
- **Banking:** A teller could help a customer rapidly and efficiently perform a reconciliation of her bank statement.

Regardless of task, content, or setting, the SME is the one who knows how to do it. The goal is to transfer their capability to one who can't do it yet. In all cases, the success criteria are always the same, measured by result, desired speed, fluency level, accuracy, or timeliness, as applicable.

The message is clear: SME, you can do it. Get me to do it. We both understand the goal. What is interfering?

Obstacles That Inhibit Transferring My Know-How to Your Know-How-To

We have insisted all along that a SME is someone who can do something. We seem to infer that expertise is a solid mixture of knowledge and performance capability. Is this true? Let's test this with the case of young Jennifer, who has the role of Gretel in the *Hansel and Gretel* ballet.

You have vast knowledge of ballet. You know the history and how it's evolved; you've seen great and poor performances, style, costuming; you understand production. Your depth of knowledge, insightful vision, and incisive commentary make you a star critic. You are a ballet SME.

I am a ballet dancer. I have performed with great success in a wide variety of ballets around the globe. I have risen to stardom and get rave reviews. I am a master of styles, and people say that how I interpret roles is brilliant. I am also a ballet SME.

But here's the question: Which one of us is better equipped to help novice ballerina Jennifer perform as Gretel—her first lead role? This is complicated. We're both experts. However, our areas of expertise are different.

Your expertise is based on observation, research, and writing about ballet as well as talking to other ballet aficionados. You possess what psychologists call declarative knowledge. On the other hand, I gained my expertise through actual dancing, continuous practice and rehearsal, and, ultimately, performance. I have deep procedural knowledge. How can we help her?

Jennifer needs help understanding the role of Gretel and how she fits into the ballet. And she has to perform the dance steps technically and make them meaningful in terms of the story.

So, let's go back to the original question. Who is better equipped to help Jennifer? The answer is both of us. Our combined expertise will help her become a wonderful dancer and the best Gretel she can be. If we both work with her, we can clearly identify her needs at each moment, clarify those needs in terms she understands, and introduce practice, with feedback, to shape her in the role. Neither of us are professional trainers. Nevertheless, we can transfer the appropriate expertise in the correct doses, just as the OTs in our previous scenarios did. We can also access rich, mediated materials—such as films with great dancers, dance clips from social media or the internet, and still images—and even visit the theater to enhance our explanations and demonstrations. This will all help Jennifer and enrich our know-how transfer.

From Our Journal

As consultants working with a variety of organizations in numerous industries, we have depended on SMEs to provide their know-how as we develop training programs. One of our favorite SMEs was a Canadian naval captain and experienced fleet commodore who led ship convoys across the ocean. His content knowledge was vast, and his passion for the work was amazing. However, it was hard for him to translate his exhaustive knowledge into words that less experienced naval officers could absorb and retain.

We worked closely with him to channel that knowledge and experience into meaningful, memorable content that his naval officers could use to acquire the know-how-to they needed to navigate with large ship convoys and make decisions that he did intuitively. Together we built a dynamic, interactive game called High Seas, which was later adopted by the US Coast Guard and NATO navies.[3]

Some Key Concepts for You to Hold on to

There are a few important notions about SMEs and learning we must keep in mind as we proceed.

- **The knowing-doing gap:** You know about ballet. I know how to dance. Unfortunately, neither of us are necessarily able to transform our personal know-hows into the other's domain of expertise. It doesn't work. The declarative and procedural memory systems may be located in our brain, but they don't communicate with each other very well. To help Jennifer become a star dancer, we will have to guide her from our expertise while encouraging her do most of the work, just as Harry guided his brother-in-law in changing the filter. Make sure to clarify expectations and draw from the learner during the guidance process. Ask her to explain who Gretel is and what her feelings and fears are. Get her to perform! How does your know-how affect how she gestures and dances? Provide support, feedback, and reinforcement as she defines her role and modifies her movements (new gestures, facial expressions, and posture). And do it all in meaningful and manageable steps.

- **Unconscious competence:** As SMEs, we are unaware of what we do when we perform expertly. That's because we don't think about what steps we take to get to the restroom or in our other daily activities. We efficiently "just do it." Think about your daily commute to and from work. Initially you had to learn the route—constantly thinking about landmarks, street names, and how many blocks to go before turning—not to mention figuring out the best streets to take on different days or times. As your expertise increased, you stopped consciously thinking about what you were doing. As SMEs, we have to factor this in as we help Jennifer.

- **Confusing verbiage:** Strange words and terms can throw off learners. Jargon, specialized references, unknown names, and objects that are familiar to the SME but alien to the learner block learning. (Will Jennifer understand when I tell her to "start in *à la seconde*" or to "*tombé, pas de bourrée, glissade, pas de chat* across the floor"?) Novelty hinders learning unless it's linked to something known. Beware of the unfamiliar!

- **Arrogance and ignorance:** The tone of a SME or the perceived attitude that "everyone knows this" or "anyone can do this" can shutdown learners and decrease their self-confidence. The same can be said for apparent amazement at what the learner does not know, expressions of disbelief about lack of background, or astonishment at learners' naiveté.

- **Learner limitations:** SMEs often do not account for learners' inexperience, missing prerequisite knowledge and skills, or unfamiliarity with the cultural or environmental context into which their newly acquired know-how will fit. (For example, the importance of job titles, fundamental etiquette rules, safety risks, dress codes, and standards.) This frequently inhibits learning and performance.

These factors and many more create serious obstacles for learning. In the earlier success examples we presented, the SMEs avoided using them. Now, we're going to post huge warning signs labeled "SME: PROCEED WITH CAUTION! GOTCHAS AHEAD."

We encourage you, as the SME-OT, to take nothing for granted. Always demonstrate that your major concern is your learner's success and you are there for them. Never assume.

Let's go over a few potential pitfalls along with suggestions for side-stepping them:

Avoid	Instead, Try
Glibly saying: • "This is easy." • "You know how to do it." • "Go ahead."	• "Does this look familiar to you?" • "Have you done this before? I'll watch and guide you."
Bluntly assuming: • "Anyone can do this. No problem."	• "Ready to try this?" • "How's it going?" • "Talk out loud as you proceed. I'll coach you."
Affirming without verifying: • "You know this and can do it." • "Let's move on."	• "Do you get it?" • "Are you ready to proceed or do you want to review, try again, or ask questions?"
Stating assertively: • "This isn't rocket science." • "Even you should get it."	Offering encouragement: • "This is an important step. You do it and I'll assist, but only if you want me to or need me."

One more note of caution: Avoid vagueness and ambiguity. Be clear and specific. The fuzzier your explanations or directions, the less likely the learner will be able to "get it." Instead, break down learning into small chunks so the learner can encounter success often and you can get them back on track if they experience difficulty along the way. Reinforce what you say with examples that are meaningful to the learner.

What Is a Learner?

We have been using the term learner for three chapters. It is time we define this word. You are the SME-OT. The person working to acquire your know-how is the learner. This is the person who will end up being able to perform through you. All learners receive, process, and ultimately transform what you provide into their own know-how-to. Your responsibility is to help them achieve that goal effectively, efficiently, and meaningfully, with the least pain and maximum independent accomplishment. The central responsibility of the learner is to attend to your guidance and engage fully. You are the prime agent of change. The learner carries the heavy load of converting what you offer them into acquired capability. For success, mutual respect is key.

We have all been learners at various times in our lives. Outside the traditional settings of school, college, and training courses in business and industry, we may have been interns, apprentices, or on-the-job trainees. In every instance, our job was to learn and be able to do what we were taught.

When was the last time you were a learner? How well did your teacher/instructor/trainer do at sharing their know-how? How well did you demonstrate that the skill and knowledge transfer occurred? Both trainer and learner have individual responsibilities in the know-how to know-how-to transfer process. Both share equally in the learner's success.

 REMEMBER THIS

Read the following statements and choose the more appropriate option in parentheses to complete each one. Then, compare your choices with ours for feedback.

1. For our purposes in this book, a SME is a person *(who possesses vast amounts of expertise/who possesses sufficient skills and relevant knowledge a learner requires)* to acquire the know-how-to to perform in a desired way.

2. Knowing how to perform *(means you can readily explain how you perform/is not enough to explain how you perform)*.

3. The greater your expertise as a SME, the greater *(the probability you can communicate with/the distance between you and)* novice learners.

4. Declarative knowledge is knowledge you can *(talk about, describe, and explain/use to do or execute a task)*.

5. I am an expert plumber. I can fix almost anything to do with plumbing. Most of my knowledge is *(declarative/procedural)*.

6. To perform well as a ballerina, Jennifer *(only requires procedural/requires procedural and declarative)* knowledge.

7. If we possess unconscious competence, we *(can/cannot)* perform expertly.

8. Novelty, characterized by something completely new and unusual to a learner, *(facilitates/can easily confuse and decrease)* learning.

9. Phrases such as "the next step should be really easy for you," usually make the novice learner more *(confident/anxious)* on a first attempt.

10. When transforming SME know-how into another's know-how-to, the ultimate responsibility for the learning resides with the *(learner/occasional trainer)*.

Now, compare your choices with ours, noting our comments or the reasoning behind our responses.

1. For our purposes in this book, a SME is a person *who possesses sufficient skills and relevant knowledge a learner requires* to acquire the know-how-to to perform in a desired way. The SME is the owner of the required know-how. The important word here is requires. So long as the person has sufficient expertise (know-how) to perform, they qualify as a SME in the OT context.

2. Knowing how to perform *is not enough to explain how you perform.* Sure, you must be able to perform. However, figuring out how to explain what you can do in a way that is comprehensible and accessible to a novice is your big challenge. This is why we wrote this book.

3. The greater your expertise as a SME, the greater *the distance between you and* novice learners. This may seem illogical, but unfortunately it's true. SMEs and novices do not process information in the same way. SMEs organize the information in their memories in larger chunks than do novices. For example, when giving directions, a SME may think, "Pull out of the parking lot and head to Route 425 South," while the novice is thinking, among other things, "Do I go right or left out of my space? Where's the parking lot exit? How do I pay to exit? Was that turn right, left, or go straight past the exit? How far is it to Route 425 South?" The difference in memory chunk size is a killer to learning. We'll cover more on this later.

4. Declarative knowledge is knowledge you can *talk about, describe, and explain*. Naming, listing, or arguing for a point of view or explaining a concept are examples of declarative knowledge in action.

5. I am an expert plumber. I can fix almost anything to do with plumbing. Most of my knowledge is procedural. Shutting down a piece of equipment is an example of *procedural* knowledge.

6. To perform well as a ballerina, Jennifer *requires procedural and declarative* knowledge. While dancing is largely procedural—steps and coordinated, precise movements in time with the music and in synchrony with the other dancers—a ballerina must also acquire declarative knowledge about ballet. She needs to know its meaning, different forms of interpretation, a huge vocabulary of ballet terms, and a vast repertoire of concepts related to the history, staging, music, costuming, and other subjects.

7. If we possess unconscious competence, we *can* perform expertly. This is what expertise is all about. The more expert we become at doing something—executing a task—the less aware we are of what we are doing. We perform each step without thinking. We progress from the conscious, think-about stage (right, left, right, twirl right twice, hold head high, shoulders back) to fluently dancing in coordination with the music and our partner without reciting each step.

8. Novelty, characterized by something completely new and unusual to a learner, *can easily confuse and decrease* learning. The newer something is to the learner—whether it's a piece of equipment, a completely unfamiliar tool, an alien form of art, or a procedure they've never seen or heard of—the more easily it will throw them off. Novelty needs to be grounded by creating links between the unknown and the familiar.

9. Phrases such as "the next step should be really easy for you," usually makes the novice learner more *anxious* on a first attempt. Building the right level of confidence, especially in the initial

stages of learning how to do something new is essential. By saying, "This is pretty simple, I'm sure you'll have no problems," you're setting up the learner for a possibly humiliating failure.

10. In transforming SME know-how into another's know-how-to, the ultimate responsibility for the learning resides with the learner. The OT must do everything they can to help the *learner* succeed. The burden of succeeding, however, rests squarely on the shoulders of the learner.

Now you're ready to confront new action challenges and put what you have learned into practice. Next is chapter 4 and its formula for structuring training success.

4

It's Not Magic: A Time-Tested Model for Structuring Training Success

In the first two chapters of this book, you discovered not only what an occasional trainer (OT) is, but that you have likely found yourself playing that role. The third chapter discussed SMEs, demonstrating how they still can stumble into barriers that prevent them from communicating clearly with novices. You also received guidance to overcome these barriers.

A Winning Formula

Wouldn't it be wonderful if there were a simple, easy-to-use formula you could apply to any training, teaching, coaching, tutoring, guiding situation? And, what if that formula worked with any type or number of learners and any content or difficulty level? What if you felt confident it would result in achieving a high probability of success?

Good news! That formula exists! The 5-Step Model for Training has a long-standing success record based on its use with thousands of learners in a wide variety of situations. It is derived from our six universals of learning research, and this chapter takes you through the model using examples and instructions on how to apply it.[4]

This model first appeared in *Telling Ain't Training*, which we initially published in 2002, and has now been used effectively in organizations worldwide for nearly 20 years. Feedback from clients and readers confirms that the model is effective and efficient in producing desired results across a wide a range of subject matter areas.

The Six Universals of Learning Research

Training is a lot like parenting—everyone has a different theory about how it works and a different method for success. And while one parenting style may work wonders on a child, it may affect another child differently. Parenting is complex and the rules are diverse. Similarly, there are many different ideas and methods surrounding how to achieve effective learning results and develop training for specific outcomes. Fortunately, there is a strong body of research underlying the teaching-learning process as well as considerable information to guide an OT in their quest to help a person acquire know-how. In know-how transfer, the results are much more predictable.

Let's start by looking at the foundation for the model, which includes the six universals from learning research:

- Why?
- What?
- Structure
- Deliberate Practice
- Feedback
- Reward

Why?

The first questions a new learner will ask consciously or unconsciously are, "Why am I learning this? What's in it for me? How does this help me?" The more clearly you, as an OT, can answer the why question, the higher the probability the learner will attend more readily and exert effort to acquire your know-how: "Oh! This makes sense. This will help me to. . . ."

Grab the learner's attention with a meaningful, beneficial rationale for what we are about to do—"start up the conveyor belt with no problems on the first try" or "produce the desired slide set easily and quickly, complete with Jerry's graphics." If learners clearly perceive personal value in what they are going to learn, they learn better. Thus the know-how to know-how-to transfer occurs more effectively. Here are some examples:

- Want the quickest, easiest route to the restroom? I can give you directions and a way to remember them.
- So, you want make a delicious tuna melt? Let's get started. Your delicious sandwich awaits you.
- You can make this electronic lathe do whatever you want if you master these six easy steps. Guaranteed success! Just look, try, practice with my help, and then perform on your own.

What?

The learner will be wondering, "What exactly am I supposed to accomplish? In specific terms, if I do what you direct, what will be the outcome?" If learners know exactly what the end goal is, there is a higher likelihood that they will achieve it.

Structure

Humans have a hard time learning new things if they do not see a meaningful pattern, logic, or structure in what they are presented with. For example, examine these two groups of symbols. Which one is easier to remember?

Try looking at each one separately. Memorize what you see. Look away. Then try to recite without peeking or errors. Time yourself for each.

When we tried this exercise with 10 people, the results were clear. For the box on the left, it took 75 seconds for those who succeeded to go from initial glance to complete recall (three individuals simply gave up). For the box on the right, everyone completed the challenge in an average of 20 seconds. What was the difference? Logic and structure. Each box had the same number of the same items. The difference was that the box on the right was more clearly and logically ordered. So, remember that the more meaningfully and logically presented the know-how, the higher the probability that the learner will "get it."

Deliberate Practice

We have often heard that practice makes perfect. This is not exactly true. We argue that we need to add the word *deliberate*. Deliberate practice is focused and systematic, compared with ordinary practice, which includes endlessly rehearsed repetitions. Deliberate practice demands attention to goals that are clearly defined and is conducted with the purpose of improving performance. It requires concentration on what needs to be corrected, examination of the result, and timely, specific feedback. Sustained, deliberate practice over time will lead to improved learning and know-how transfer.

Feedback

This is information that flows back to a source, letting it know whether what is happening is on or off target. The term originated in cybernetics in which an objective is set and actions to achieve the target are triggered. The information that flows back lets us know if those actions caused the desired result or if they need to be modified.

Let's demonstrate using a thermostat. You set the temperature to 83 degrees and the furnace goes on. When the room temperature reaches that setting, a signal is sent to turn off the furnace until the temperature drops below 83 degrees again, thus triggering the thermostat to turn on the furnace until the room returns to the goal temperature. In the transfer of know-how to know-how-to, you set an objective and actions are triggered. Once the objective is reached, as verified by feedback, the training actions cease. Feedback, derived from learner results, is essential for improving learning until each objective is met. The learner deliberately practices and receives feedback, which either guides them to modify the action in a specific way or maintain the action because it is right on target.

Feedback must be specific, timely, supportive, and, above all, meaningful to the learner. Let's look at some feedback offered by a bartender OT sharing her know-how with a novice:

- "Now, place your drink next to the color chart. Does the drink's color match the recommended shade? What specific change do you need to make to deepen the shade?" (Notice that the OT's feedback asks the novice to recommend a modification first. This helps guide the new bartender to think before acting.)
- "Notice the color gradations in the display line of bottles. Are any out of sequence? Rearrange any bottle that is darker than the one to its left. Structure the line to flow in a continuous sequence from lighter to increasingly darker shades."
- "Great! You've correctly matched each wine with the appropriate type of glass. Keep checking the wine glass chart to maintain your awesome record."

Reward

It is motivating for a person attempting to acquire your know-how to be informed that their actions or responses are correct. Letting learners know they are on the right path and "getting it," reinforces the knowledge and increases the probability of continuously improved performance.

Disapproval, negative remarks, and even punishing behaviors or comments will produce unpredictable results. Rewards through words, tone of voice, or actions generate increased success.

A final word on the six universals—the research findings have remained stable over a long period of time. They can generally be trusted to guide successful know-how transfer.

The 5-Step Model for Structuring and Conducting Know-How Training

From the six universals, we can now create an easy-to-apply model for helping any OT, whether accidental or assigned, develop know-how-to capability in others.

Let's first examine the model in its graphic form.

THE 5-STEP MODEL

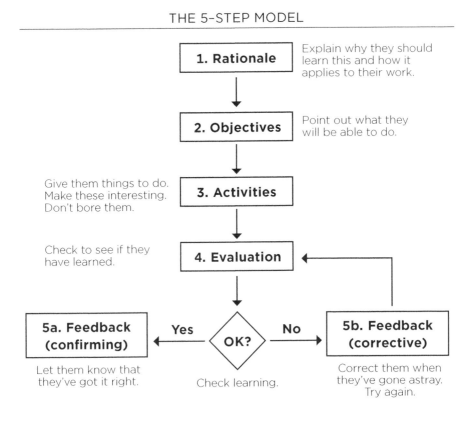

Now, we'll elaborate using an example in which you are a supermarket OT cashier, helping a customer acquire the capability to use self-checkout.

Step	Actions	Example
1. Rationale	Establish a clear, meaningful reason for learning how to do this. Emphasize for the learner, "What's in it for me? What's the value and benefit."	"So, you hate wasting time standing in long checkout lines. Wouldn't it be great if you could cut your wait time in half and get on with your life? It's really easy to do if we do it together. Let's try."
2. Objective	Clearly and specifically state what the learner will accomplish by sticking with you and participating in the actions that follow.	"I'm going to guide you as you check yourself out. By the time we're done, you'll be able to scan your shopping items, check for price accuracy, fill your shopping bags, pay, and leave . . . all in just a few minutes."
3. Activities	Quickly engage the learner in a logical set of activities. You should direct and guide while the learner follows along.	"First, look at the screen in front of you. Notice the word 'START.' What should you do? Good! Press that button and see what appears. Read the message. What should you do now? Great!"
4. Evaluation	Continue guiding the learner's actions as you observe each step. Verify their performance is correct and keep checking for accuracy. Did the learner get it or not?	Watch the learner's actions and the screen at each step. Did they place the item on the scanner correctly? Did it register? Was the item removed immediately and placed in a shopping bag?

| 5. Feedback | Each time your learner responds or acts, let them know if they are on or off target. Either correct any deviation or confirm success. Make sure your feedback is stated positively, even if it is corrective. When necessary, explain or point out what needs to be altered. Draw suggestions from the learner about how to do better and have them try again. Work together to obtain the desired result and confirm by adding a reinforcing statement. | "When you positioned your item on the scanner, did you notice that the price and item didn't appear on the screen? Why do you think that happened? Good, you noticed the bar code wasn't facing the scanner. What should you do? Great! Now there's the item along with the price. Bravo! Now, remove the item from the scanner and bag it. Watch out for that going forward." |

In applying the model, the dialogue and activities should flow naturally and fluently. Make sure that the learner can perform independently and confidently by the end. And make sure they have information about how to get assistance the next time they try it out alone.

As you engage in know-how transfer using the 5-Step model, remember that:

- The model requires continuous learner involvement, participation, and practice.
- The responsibility for achieving success resides with the learner, who must continually engage and demonstrate successful performance by applying appropriate behaviors and achieving the successful outcomes.
- As the OT, you set the stage, drive the learning events, insert examples, guide progress, provide feedback, and reinforce or reward results.

Application of the 5-Step Model

Take a look at the complete case scenario presenting the 5-Step model in action that follows. Do not simply read the scenario. Put yourself into it. Imagine you are there.

AT THE FAIR

OT:
As a ticket seller, one of your most important tasks will be to tell attendees the exact price of the tickets they are requesting. When the fair is busy, lines can be long and customers can get impatient. You've got to be fast and accurate. Slowness and errors could create anger and scenes. Do you want that? I guessed not.

Now, your booth only serves customers buying up to eight adult tickets and any combination of child and senior tickets up to eight. If they need more than that they'll need to go to a group sales booth. So, wouldn't you love to know the exact price for any combination of adult, senior, and child tickets in seconds? No pressure on you and no fuss?

New Hire:
Absolutely! But aren't there different prices for each category? What if someone asks for 2 adult, 2 senior, and 3 child tickets? It can get complicated calculating the total with all the noise and confusion around you.

OT:
You're right. But what if you had a sure-fire tool to help you always be accurate and fast?

New Hire:
Bring it on!

OT:
OK. By the end of our session, you'll be able to quote the price of any combination of tickets up to 8 adults and 8 child-senior combo in 10 seconds or less with 100 percent accuracy. Ready for the challenge?

New Hire:
Sure. . . . I guess???

OT: I give you the Ticket Charge Chart!

		\multicolumn{9}{c}{**Number of Adult Tickets**}

		0	**1**	**2**	**3**	**4**	**5**	**6**	**7**	**8**
Number of Special Tickets	**0**	0	23	46	69	82	115	138	161	184
	1	12	35	58	81	94	127	150	173	196
	2	24	47	70	93	106	139	162	185	208
	3	36	59	82	105	118	151	174	197	220
	4	48	71	**94**	117	130	163	186	209	232
	5	60	83	106	129	142	172	198	221	244
	6	72	95	118	141	154	187	210	233	256
	7	84	107	130	153	166	199	222	245	268
	8	96	119	142	165	178	211	234	257	280

An adult ticket is $23. A child's ticket is $12. A senior ticket is also $12. Look at the chart. If a customer asks for 2 adult, 3 child, and 1 senior ticket, you would place your right index finger on the number 2 under Number of Adult Tickets. Then, move your finger down the column to the row for 4 special tickets (3 child and 1 senior). The number in the box (column for 2 adults, row for 4 special) indicates that the total combined price is $94. Well done!

		\multicolumn{9}{c}{**Number of Adult Tickets**}

		0	**1**	**2**	**3**	**4**	**5**	**6**	**7**	**8**
Number of Special Tickets	**0**	0	23	46	69	82	115	138	161	184
	1	12	35	58	81	94	127	150	173	196
	2	24	47	70	93	106	139	162	185	208
	3	36	59	82	105	118	151	174	197	220
	4	48	71	94	117	130	163	186	209	232
	5	60	83	106	129	142	172	198	221	244
	6	72	95	118	141	154	187	210	233	256
	7	84	107	130	153	166	199	222	245	268
	8	96	119	142	165	178	211	234	257	280

OT:	Now, let's try three more customer requests. You've got 10 seconds for each. I'll time you!
	• 1 adult and 8 child
	• 4 adult, 4 child, and 3 senior
	• 7 senior

New Hire:	I got $184, $166, and $84.

OT:	Fantastic! You just made one error when you chose $184 for the first one. Can you show me what you did? Aha! Notice you chose 1 adult, but then moved over horizontally to 8 adult tickets? What should you have done?

New Hire:	Oh, I see. I should have moved my finger vertically down the 1 adult column to 8 special tickets for $119 total. Big goof.

OT:	Nice catch! Now, practice by inventing a few customer requests and coming up with the right totals. Excellent. You're catching on quickly. You got them all right and each under 10 seconds, even with a self-correct. You are headed toward job success with minimal stress.
	Are you ready to move on to the next challenge—collecting money (cash or credit) and making change? You have done really well so far. Keep practicing with your chart. You can always call on me with questions.

To conclude, for the moment, on the 5-Step model, take a minute to practice applying it completely on your own using the worksheet we created. Use the following know-how to know-how-to scenario or one of your own to try out the model. The worksheet makes you think through each step of the 5-step process, collect your ideas, and examine what you have written. As you become comfortable with the model, which is simply a way of structuring your OT thinking, you will begin to apply it intuitively.

 ## SCENARIO: BE SAFE

You work as a bellhop at a resort hotel where guests visit from around the world. One of your jobs is to ensure that your guests can operate the in-room safe perfectly and independently. It can be very unpleasant if a tired traveler is unable to retrieve something from the safe in the middle of the night, can't operate it in the morning as they are hurrying to catch a tour, or forget how to lock it and leave with the safe unlocked. You know how to make the safe work. You must pass on this know-how to your hotel guests so they can successfully operate the safe.

Using the worksheet below, enter the key points of what to say and do, and have the hotel guest learners do, as you transform your know-how into their know-how-to.

5-STEP KNOW-HOW WORKSHEET

		Self-Check
Rationale	(List the reasons you will present to draw in the learner.)	❑ Clear learner benefit ❑ What's in it for me? ❑ Reasons for the learner to engage
Objective	(State exactly what the learner will be able to do.) When we have finished, you will be able to. . . .	❑ State in terms of the learner ❑ Specific and verifiable ❑ Meaningful to the learner
Activities	(List the learning events. What will you do and what will the learner do to store valuables or documents, lock, and unlock the safe?)	❑ In logical sequence for learner ❑ Engaging; interactive ❑ Leads to objective attainment
Evaluation	(What will you do to verify that the learner has successfully accomplished each step?)	❑ Listen to the learner ❑ Observe learner performance ❑ Verify learner success
Feedback	(How you will provide corrective or confirming feedback?)	❑ Help learner note errors ❑ Positively present corrective feedback ❑ Learner corrected errors ❑ Confirm and reinforce learner success

Use the worksheet as an outline to plan your know-how transfer session with the hotel guests. It will help you structure your thinking and guide your actions. Mentally rehearse it or role play with a friend and then debrief. You can make up the actions for setting the safe combination and making it work, but keep it simple.

Congratulations on trying the 5-Step model. Remember: Deliberate practice makes perfect.

REMEMBER THIS

We've reached the end of a chapter! As before, review each statement and select the option best suited to make the statement accurate. On completion, compare your selections with ours.

1. The first learning research universal finding can be summarized as (*"Why? How does this benefit me"/"Why? Why is so much effort necessary?"*)

2. The (*rationale/objective*) states what the novice learner will be able to do once the OT has transformed their know-how into the learner's know-how-to.

3. Deliberate practice requires (*endless repetition and rehearsal/focus on specific performance goals and practice with feedback*).

4. In the 5-Step model, feedback comes in two varieties: (*positive and negative/confirming and corrective*).

5. The use of (*a mixture of rewards and punishments/rewards*) is valuable for improving performance success.

6. The 5-Step model includes (*rationale, objectives, activities, evaluation, and feedback/rationale, objectives, explanations, evaluation, and feedback*).

7. "When you pressed the START button, nothing happened. Now watch what happens when you use two hands—one to press the blue switch and the other to hit START." This is an example of (*confirming/corrective*) feedback.

8. Application of the 5-Step model (*guarantees/increases the probability of*) know-how transfer success.

Compare your selections with ours.

1. The first learning research universal finding can be summarized as *"Why? How does this benefit me?"* When the learner sees how valuable the OT's know-how is if mastered, the probability of learning success increases.

2. The *objective* states what the novice learner will be able to do once the OT has transformed their own know-how into the learner's know-how-to. Objectives are the statements that clarify the accomplishment resulting from the learning activities. Objective attainment can always be observed and measured in some overt way.

3. Deliberate practice requires *focus on specific performance goals and practice with feedback.* Deliberate practice is different from endless repetition—it is centered on continuous improvement.

4. In the 5-Step model, feedback comes in two varieties: *confirming and corrective.* Positive and negative combined with feedback are terms used in other contexts and are less meaningful than confirming (You got it!) and corrective (let's see why you didn't get it and what you can do achieve the desired result) during know-how acquisition.

5. The use of *rewards* is valuable for improving learning and performance success. The use of punishment in word or action is shown to have very mixed results in terms of learning and performance improvement.

6. The 5-Step model is *rationale, objectives, activities, evaluation, and feedback.* Activities imply many forms of engagement. Providing explanations can be activities, but there are so many other possibilities. Remember: The more the learner is actively engaged, the more they will learn and the greater their motivation to use it.

7. "When you pressed the START button, nothing happened. Now what happens when you use both hands—one to press the blue button and the other to hit START." This is an example

of *corrective* feedback, which is guidance to act in a manner that produces a successful outcome.

8. Application of the 5-Step model *increases the probability of* know-how transfer success. Nothing guarantees success. However, the model helps improve the chances that a learner will get it.

This chapter focused on structuring your know-how transformation sessions through thoughtful planning and applying research-based rules that work for OTs. Now, the rubber hits the road. Let's get out there and start training. Fasten your seatbelt and prepare to hit some bumps!

Don't Touch, Don't Tell, and the 50/50 Rule

This short chapter highlights a few fundamental lessons for the OT. It stands alone because these lessons deal with the heart and soul of effective know-how transfer. Let's begin with a brief scene and then discuss what occurred.

THE SCREENSHOT

Novice: I'm stuck at this point in my work. I need to put a copy of this PowerPoint slide into this manual I'm writing in MS Word. Is there a way to do that without printing the PowerPoint image onto a sheet of paper and physically pasting that image on a page where I've printed my text?

OT: Sure! It's called capturing a screenshot. All you have to do is select your screen, hit the print screen button, and paste the image into your manual, size it down, select how you want to mix the image and text, and away you go. . . .

Novice: Wow! That sounds great, I think, but I've never done anything like that before. Can you teach me how?

OT: No problem. Here, let me show you. Watch. So, first I pull up the screen I want to replicate. See? Then, I hit the print screen button, which sends the image to the clipboard. Notice that it only took a couple of seconds? Then I go to the manual page in MS Word and click here to position my cursor. Got that? Watch what happens when I hit paste. Voilà! There's the image. How big do you want it to be in the manual? I can reduce or increase the image size with my cursor, then position it on the manual page like so.

Novice: Wow! That's so neat. How did you do that so fast? Can you show me again?

OT: What's the matter? Weren't you following? Didn't you see how easy it was to transfer the image? Watch me resize the image, position it, and set the image-text mix to establish how you want them to work together.

 QUICK
ACTIVITY

Answer the questions below by circling your choice for each:

Who did most of the work?	OT	Novice
Did the OT verify the Novice's prior knowledge?	Yes	No
Did the OT engage the active participation of the learner?	Yes	No
What was the Novice's primary activity?	Watch	Act
To this point, has the Novice learned how to perform?	Yes	No
If the OT continues like this will the OT's know-how become the Novice's know-how-to?	Yes	No
What went wrong? Let's discuss.		

We bet that your answers to the first six questions will match ours. We answered OT, No, No, Watch, No, and No. We also bet that we'll agree about what went wrong, and that if this form of instruction (attempt at know-how transfer) continues, the Novice will come away with little practical capability to perform.

The scene clearly showed that the OT, with the best intentions, basically took over. Saying "here, let me show you; watch" may sound friendly and helpful, but these words are know-how transfer killers. Avoid them at all costs. We have a computer technician who has tried to do this with us for years, and we stop him every time he takes charge. Yes, he is the SME. We know that he wants to make it easy for us. However, as an OT, your job is not to tell. It is to help the learner do.

Here are two possible responses an OT could give to the Novice's request of "Can you teach me?":

- "Sure. Just sit here beside me and observe while I do it and explain my actions."
- "Sure. So you want to transfer an image of a PowerPoint slide to a page in MS Word and add explanatory text. Is that right? Thanks for confirming the goal. Let's begin. You're going to do the steps as I guide you through them and observe your actions. Don't worry; I'll assist as necessary."

Which approach do you think will better transfer the OT's know-how to the Novice's know-how-to?

We choose the second option. In the first, the OT takes over and tells. In the second, the OT confirms the Novice's desired goal and establishes the appropriate roles for each of them in the transfer process: The Novice acts while the OT guides, observes, and assists as necessary.

This leads us to the two most important lessons of know-how transfer:

- No telling
- No touching

The Two Biggest Don'ts in Transforming Your Know-How Into Another Person's Know-How-To

No Telling

Avoid telling the learner everything about the task at hand, how it will work, what steps you will take, and on and on. Once you establish the desired end result (reproduce the PowerPoint slide in the manual, resize, and add text) and a learner-centered rationale, you can immediately engage the learner in doing something. Ask questions to establish the learner's relevant background and experience (Are you familiar with the keyboard? Show me the print screen key.). Do not list off the steps that will occur along the way (just select your screen, hit the print screen button, paste it into your manual, size it, and select how you want to mix the image). Cut to the chase!

No Touching

Touching refers to taking over and doing it yourself—pressing keys, hitting buttons, or flipping switches—rather than letting the learner do it. No saying, "Let me demonstrate how to do it," unless there is an element of danger involved! Stay hands off as much as possible. Let learners do all the holding, switching, and pressing. If you are helping with directions, point to a map or drawing, but let the learners point to landmarks or street names. Identify objects in their environment and have them note those as cues. Question them frequently and provide corrective or confirming feedback.

Let's look at another example.

GETTING AROUND MANHATTAN

Visitor: Excuse me. Do you know your way around Manhattan?

You: Sure. Where are you headed?

Visitor: We want to get to Hell's Kitchen Park. Is it far? Can we walk?

You: It's pretty close. About 10 minutes by foot.

Visitor: Great! How do we get there?

You: Hell's Kitchen Park, right? Good. Do you know where you are now?

Visitor: At the entrance of the Renaissance Hotel on Seventh Avenue.

You: Excellent. Step outside and look right. Notice the street sign? What does it say?

Visitor: Uhhhh. . . . 47th Street West.

You: Right, now walk to the corner. If you keep going, the street numbers go down: 47th Street, 46th Street. From the corner of Seventh Avenue and 47th Street, turn right. As you walk up 47th Street, the avenue will numbers go up. So, after you turn the corner what will be the next avenue?

Visitor: We're on Seventh Avenue so, Eighth, I guess.

You: Right! Keep on going; what's next? And next?

Visitor: Ninth. . . . 10th. . . .

You: Right on. Keep walking until you reach 10th Ave. Then, turn right and walk about 100 feet. Look right and you'll be facing Hell's Kitchen Park! OK, let's do a final check—tell me what you're going to do to get there.

Visitor: Go out the hotel door, turn right to get to corner of 47th Street and Seventh Avenue, turn right and walk straight up to 10th Avenue, turn right and walk 100 feet. Look right to face the park. Easy!

You: You've got it. Here's a rough map to help refresh your memory. Notice that I put in an arrow from the hotel saying, "street numbers down" and one at the 47th Street corner saying, "avenue numbers up," to help you get around. Enjoy your visit!

Visitor Hotel door, turn right, corner, turn right, 10th Avenue turn right, 100 feet, look right. Bingo! Fantastic! Thanks.

Note that you asked the Visitor to contribute their prior knowledge, state what they observed, and infer correct answers. The Visitor was continuously engaged while you guided, observed, and gave feedback. You even shared a job aid in the form of a sketch for reference in case of forgetfulness. Best of all, you boosted the Visitor's confidence in getting around Manhattan. Well done!

From Our Personal Journal

We both have Apple watches. When we started using them, we found it difficult to keep our hands off the other one's watch. Why? It just seemed faster and easier to grab the other person's watch and demonstrate how to do something, rather than lead our partner through the steps to acquire capability on "how to do it" using patient guidance with feedback. We lost perspective in our excitement over our new watches and forgot our own rules for helping one another learn!

So, we asked ourselves, "What will happen when I have to perform that action again or a similar one? Will I know what to do? Will we be able to replicate the steps or generalize the actions to new instances?" When we stopped to test each other it became evident that we had done a poor training job. We decided to start over. This time when we applied what we teach others, we began to retain more and perform better.

The moral of this story? Even so-called learning specialists can forget what it takes to ensure know-how transfer takes place. Full of enthusiasm, we got carried away with "Let me show you." We have humbly learned our lesson.

Don't I Sometimes Have to Tell, Touch, or Intervene in Some Way?

Reluctantly, we say "Yes, occasionally." Never is a strong word. However, you should also recognized that it's tempting to step in too soon if the learner is struggling. Give them the most opportunity to try things out. You can tell or touch if learners are experiencing mounting frustration, but then make sure they immediately practice by themselves. Reward gradual successes. The goal is for them to acquire independent capability.

A few examples follow:

- I can't get the corkscrew to go in completely. I can't get the cork out. And now I can't even pull the corkscrew out myself!!
  - All right. Let's work together. Watch as I remove the corkscrew slowly. Notice how I'm twisting it side to side a very little at a time as I gently angle the corkscrew to stand up straighter. Here, you take a turn. Mimic what I did, slowly. I'll take a turn, then you. Aim to correct the angle to straight up.
  - Now let's figure out what initially went wrong. Why don't you suggest a way to avoid the problem, and I'll follow your guidance? If I run into difficulties, we can discuss solutions. I'll try the solution. Then we'll reverse roles.
- The car keeps stalling every time I release the clutch and press on the gas pedal. I'll never learn how to drive a manual gearshift car.
  - Relax. With the engine off, you already demonstrated how to depress the clutch with your left foot as you move your stick from the center neutral position up and to the top left to get into first gear. You just showed me how to depress the clutch and smoothly pull the stick down to the bottom left to shift into second. For third gear, now depress the clutch and move diagonally to the top right. For fourth gear, hit the clutch and smoothly pull the stick down to the bottom right. Let's review the actions one more time.
  - Wonderful. Now, I'm changing seats with you and moving to the driver's side. Watch my feet.
- I still can't open the jam jar, even with the rubber grip. I tried twice doing what you suggested.
  - I noticed that both times you jerked hard as you twisted left. Watch as I slowly twist with force—no jerking. Did you see how the lid moved bit by bit and finally came off? Here's another jar that you can try. Slow and steady. . . . Yes! You did it like a pro.

Bottom line: Get in if all else fails, demonstrate and explain, but make sure you're continuously engaging the learner. Share activities as much as possible. Get the learners back in the saddle and performing immediately and independently.

The 50/50 Rule

When we observe trainers in action, the trainer— whether full-time, occasional, or accidental—often appears to be speaking and doing most of the time. Not good. Especially in know-how transfer. Our rule of thumb is that the learner should be doing and talking at least 50 percent of the time. Note the  "at least." More than 50 percent is even better. The learner should be doing, acting, speaking, puzzling out, practicing, or responding half or more of the training-learning time.

The more learners do what is meaningful to them, the more they learn. Conversely, the less they do, the less they learn. In our work evaluating trainers delivering courses within organizations and one-on-one coaching, when monitoring, guiding feedback, and coaching trainers maintaining that 50/50 relationship consistently requires the most attention.

Our advice? Get out of the learner's way. To be most effective, the OT should be the guide on the side, not the sage on the stage. This an old saying whose origins are unknown, but the message remains relevant.[5]

MOM, I WANT TO BE JUST LIKE YOU

Jenny:	Wow, Mom! I love this toy remote-control excavator. It's exactly what I wanted. It looks just like the one you operate in your work. Can you teach me how to operate it like you do your real one?
Mom:	Sure. What do you want to be able to do?
Jenny:	I guess power it up, drive it around, dig holes and ditches in the ground, umm . . . climb tough hills, pick up heavy stuff with the shovel, grab tree branches, and drain water from a hole.

Mom: That's quite a lot! It took me a really long time to learn how to do all of that with a real excavator. Why don't we start by powering up? Then we can try driving. And then digging holes? Let's take our time and make sure you can do each task well.

Jenny: Okay, I guess. Power up. Then, driving. Then, digging up holes to start.

Mom: To make it work, what will you have to do first?

Jenny: Start her up.

Mom: What does a car need for it to work?

Jenny: Gas!

Mom: Right on! But this excavator actually works on electricity. You have to charge the battery from a power pack that you plug into the wall. Let's figure out how to fill her up with electric fuel. Look at the plans and all the parts shown on them. Do you see something that says charger? And what part on the drawing says Power plug in?

Jenny: Look! There's the charger drawing. Here's the charger with a power cord and plug. That must go into the wall outlet and the other cord has a round plug for the excavator. Can I plug them both in?

Mom: OK, but I'm watching. Remember the most important rule?

Together: Safety first!

Mom: So, be extra careful. This is electricity. Tell me what you're about to do. Then, at my signal, do it. (Mom observes as Jenny proceeds carefully.)

Well done! Now we'll have to wait a bit until the excavator's power light changes from red to green.

Jenny: The power light is on red. It's fueling up. This is fun! I can't wait to become an operator like you, Mom!

Check off in this session what you noticed.

Y	N	
☐	☐	Did Jenny react positively to her new present?
☐	☐	Did Jenny's mom (the OT) verify Jenny's desired outcome?
☐	☐	Did Mom and Jenny set mutually agreed-upon know-how transfer objectives?
☐	☐	Did Mom ask guiding questions to help Jenny formulate next steps?
☐	☐	Did Mom dictate what the sequence of events had to be?
☐	☐	Did Mom draw out the sequence of events from Jenny?
☐	☐	Did Mom select the charger and plug-in port for Jenny to point out their locations?
☐	☐	Did Jenny activate the power charging?
☐	☐	Did Mom congratulate Jenny on her safe behavior?
☐	☐	Did Jenny do most of the work?

 REMEMBER
THIS

This chapter focused on a few essential rules for effective know-how transfer. Review the following statements and select an option from each parenthetical pair, then check your choices against ours.

1. Transforming your know-how to another's know-how-to is active and intense. In this process, the (*OT/learner*) should be doing the most work.

2. If the OT begins the know-how transfer process by (*explaining, demonstrating and listing the main steps/getting the learner to engage and act*) up front, the know-how transfer result will be more effective.

3. For the OT, no touching means (*never touch the learner/do not take over and start demonstrating the actions to be performed*).

4. The OT should (*never/only*) tell, touch, or intervene if the learner truly cannot perform.

5. A good ratio of OT to Novice learner activity in a know-how transfer session is (*80/20 / 50/50*).

6. An old but still valid adage for training is for the trainer to be the (*sage on the stage/guide on the side*).

Here is how we responded:

1. Transforming your know-how to another's know-how-to is active and intense. In this process, the *learner* should be doing the most work. The responsibility for achieving learning success or acquiring the know-how-to resides with learner. The more the learner does, the more they learn.

2. If the OT begins the know-how transfer process by *getting the learner to engage and act* up front, the know-how transfer result will be more effective. Tell less. Get the learner doing immediately.

3. For the OT, no touching means *do not take over and start demonstrating the actions to be performed.* In this context, the no touching rule refers to hands off the switches, tools, and other objects requiring manipulation. Get the learner's fingers and hands working. Let the learner say and do.

4. The OT should *only* tell, touch, or intervene if the learner truly cannot perform. A bit of struggle and challenge is good for the learner. Only after they have observed sincere effort, provided feedback, and noticed that learner's frustration is mounting should the OT step in to demonstrate and assist. Then, the learner must take over and try again.

5. A good ratio of OT to Novice learner activity in a know-how transfer session is *50/50.* Like a good conversation, balance is desirable. In know-how transfer, tipping the ratio to more learner action can be even better.

6. An old but still valid adage for training is for the trainer to be the *guide on the side.* We believe that the saying speaks for itself.

The next chapter is a meaty one and focuses on practice. Consistent, deliberate practice leads to long-term retention and fluent performance. There is a lot in the chapter, including practice for you.

Practice! Practice! Practice!

CHAPTER HIGHLIGHTS:

- Why can I do so many things quickly, without thinking, and still get them right?
- How a person learns *physiologically*—how the body naturally does it.
- Three important learning facts.
- Stress—its effects on learning and stress reduction.
- Training strategies that build learner confidence and success.
- Techniques for enhancing practice and repetition.

READY FOR A CHALLENGE?

Get out your timer (use your smartphone, stopwatch, watch, or computer). When you're ready, start the timer and begin filling in the blanks to the questions below as fast as you can. Do not peek before starting the challenge. As soon as you've filled in the last blank, stop the clock. The goal is to complete them all in less than 30 seconds. Ready? Go!

A B __ D __ F G __ I __ K __ M __ __ __ Q R S __ U V __ X __ Z

$8 \times 5 =$ ___ $7 \times 7 =$ ___ $4 \times 9 =$ ___ $3 \times 6 =$ ___

Note your time here: ___

Most people can complete this activity in less than 30 seconds or very close to it. When we tried it, one of us did it in 18 seconds, the other in 13. (She was faster.) Why are we so fast and accurate? Because we were drilled in the alphabet and the multiplication tables as kids. The answers have become *automatic*. No thinking, just responding.

Another way of explaining this is that we learned through lots of practice.

Three Important Facts About Learning

The use of practice in transferring know-how has been well-studied. Let's highlight three important findings that are helpful for you as an OT.

- **Learning is not easy.** We are genetically coded—hardwired, you could say—to learn. This is good, isn't it? Yes, but it's not so simple. The key is the brain, which has evolved over millions of years. However, the brain has not yet caught up with the ever-increasing demands of our rapidly changing industrial, technological world. Learning occurs when connections are made by neurons in the brain. Each one possesses thin threadlike axons that carry electrical signals to the connecting dendrites of other neurons. It is like a messaging system—our senses pick out a sound, taste, or image and send it to our brain cells, passing the message on from axon to dendrite. These connections allow learning to occur. Other types of brain cells monitor the axons for activity and release chemicals to produce a substance called myelin around the activated axons. The A Note About Our Brain section below provides a bit more scientific explanation if you are curious. If not, skip it and continue. You can also find tons of information on the internet about how learning takes place.

- **Persistent, repeated practice and rehearsal increase learning and decrease effort to retain.** This takes time, which, in our overwhelmingly demanding world, is in short supply.
- **Deliberate practice that focuses on correcting and reinforcing highly specific, targeted learning and performance goals improves learning speed and retention.** Practice that repeats errors reduces the reinforcement of connections at the synapse, resulting in weaker myelination and decreased speed and strength of the desired result.

A Note About the Brain

All your senses—sight, hearing, smell, touch, and taste—have sensors that connect you to the world around you. When information bombards your senses, they sort through the array of messages, filter what gets through and what gets left out, and send the relevant signals along to your brain. Then your brain cells start to do the thinking work: Neuronal cells pass information along from the axons, or threadlike tendrils of the neuron to other threadlike tendrils called dendrites, which connect with the axons of other neuronal cells. (Of course this all happens lightning fast.) The junction between where a dendrite and axon meet is called a synapse. Other cells called astrocytes monitor axons for activity. When any activity is detected, astrocytes release chemicals that stimulate oligodendrocyte cells to produce myelin around the activated axons.

This process, called myelination, produces an ever-thickening coating around the activated axons, which accelerates the speed and improves the strength of the learning connection. When the brain is observed using high-resolution imaging, like an f-MRI scanner, we can actually see chemical evidence of learning taking place.

 REPEAT, REPEAT, REPEAT

There is an English word that begins with letter R and means a repeated pattern of sound. In music it refers to the song's beat; it is what we dance to. If you know this word, write it in the box below. Then cover it.

The other thing about this word is that it isn't easy to spell. So, let's fix that. Keep the word covered and repeat the following five sentences out loud.

Say the covered word each time as the first word of the sentence. Use the first letter of each word that follows as spelling clues:

R_____ helps your two hips move.
R_____ helps your two hips move.
R_____ helps your two hips move.
R_____ helps your two hips move.
R_____ helps your two hips move.

Please correctly spell the covered word: _____.

Did you spell rhythm correctly both times or only after you repeated the five sentences?

If you already knew the correct spelling, then there was no problem. Bravo! However, if you spelled it incorrectly the first time, we bet you corrected yourself on the second attempt. The repetitive nature of the sentence, "Rhythm helps your two hips move," almost always leads to better accuracy and less hesitation. Try this exercise with a few friends.

The purpose is to demonstrate that precise, deliberate, and consistent practice produces faster, better learning and retention.

How Stress Affects Learning

Do you think stress affects how well a person absorbs know-how from another person? Research suggests that stress can adversely affect memory and learning with negative consequences for retention and performance. Improper training can increase the negative effects.[6]

In training, several factors can trigger stress: for example, the context, the consequences, the learner, or the OT. Even the environment can build anxiety if there is risk, high unfamiliarity, demand, or pressure beyond the learner's experience; multiple sensory distractors such as noise, darkness, crowds, or too much going on; or excessive responsibility. The consequences of not "getting it" or not performing to expectations can freak out the learner, increase the possibility of injury (oneself or others), or increase the cost or damage as a result of poor performance. Learners can even create their own internal stress sources if they're prone to becoming anxious and stressed by almost anything. The OT's words, body language, facial expression, or lack of useful, timely and clear direction or feedback can directly produce learner stress.

Scientifically speaking, when stress factors manifest themselves, the learner's adrenal glands (which are located just above the kidneys) release a hormone called cortisol. The positive effect of cortisol is that it whips the individual to high alert—muscles tighten, focus sharpens, energy increases, and oxygen flow improves. They're ready for action. However, too much cortisol can cause a build-up of anxiety, loss of clear thought, disrupted ability to speak or act productively, and an overall breakdown in learning and performance. You may know this as the "fight or flight response."

For those who are naturally anxious, this cortisol overdose can occur quickly. It's up to the OT to help reduce the negative effects and shore up the positives.

How OTs Reduce Learner Stress and Improve Learning and Performance

Let's look at what you can do as an occasional trainer to reduce the effects of heightened stress:

- Before starting, select the learning environment with care. Reduce any noise and distracting or stimulating elements that aren't essential for learning. For example, if you are training ticket sellers at a noisy, crowded fair, start by introducing the essentials, tools, and steps in a quiet environment. Once the learner can perform in a non-overwhelming atmosphere, gradually add audio and visual distractions (for example, use speakers to play increasingly louder audio recordings, people circulating, interruptions, and so forth). Use simulation to approach reality.

- Explain the importance of the knowledge transfer and its consequences while reassuring the learner that many have learned how to do this. Provide tricks and cues for spotting a possible mishap and how to recover quickly. Use job aids and decision tables to avoid the consequences of an error. Try these two examples for avoiding negative effects of an error:
  - The learner entered the wrong information for a credit transaction. Using the job aid you provided, ask the learner to cancel the credit card transaction. Then have them follow the steps in the job aid to re-enter the transaction correctly. Observe, provide guidance and feedback, and reward successful performance. Repeat and practice as needed.
  - The learner selected the wrong ingredient (ugh!) to add to cake batter while following the recipe. Always observe as the learner practices. Have them speak aloud (a frequently used training technique) what they are about to do before they do it. Ask them questions: Why this ingredient? What does it do? Examine the recipe and the ingredient. Taste it. Discuss and provide feedback.

- To reduce learner-induced stress, ask, "How are you feeling right now?" Probe for feelings of uncertainty or inadequacy. Discuss the reasons for these feelings. Recommend taking some relaxing breaths. Have the learner say what they are about to do; rehearse the steps in their mind; break the sequence into small chunks; and repeat with actions, reinforcing successes. Reward successful completion. Then repeat! Remind the learner of the success and refer to it later when faced with another challenge.

- To avoid stressing the learner out:
  ◦ Anticipate challenges from the learner's perspective and reassure them.
  ◦ Break the transfer of know-how from you to your learner into small chunks, making sure to include lots of practice, feedback, and reward. Proceed at the pace of your learner.
  ◦ Focus your feedback on the learner's performance and never on the learner. Say: "You can still see lumps in the batter. What can you do to eliminate them? Good. Try it." Do not say: "You left lumps in the batter. You didn't whip it long enough. Not good."
  ◦ Be supportive and encouraging. Watch your words, tone, facial expressions, gestures, and even body language. Do everything possible to show the learner that you are on their side. Let them know that their success is your success.

Two Training Strategies to Build Learner Confidence and Success

We find that the Teach–Prompt–Release strategy and the Teach Me strategy help reduce learner stress and build their confidence.

Teach—Prompt—Release

This is a simple way of thinking about what you are supposed to do as you train a novice. The process focuses on eliciting the correct response and reinforcing correct outcomes.

- **Teach.** Initiate the session or interaction. Define the goal, as we have said before. Get the learner to observe, act, and repeat. Become involved as you guide by encouraging and providing feedback that draws out the correct response. You take charge as the learner begins to practice.

- **Prompt.** Once the learner starts to do things on their own, your role shifts to being a feedback provider and prompter. Only intervene as necessary—a hint here, a cue there, a comment or quick question, and a reward for accomplishment. That's it.
- **Release.** Finally, when you see that learners can "do it," release them to fly solo. Like a parent bird, stick around to monitor as feasible. However, your charge must take flight. The good news is that you still leave behind something the learner can refer to as necessary, such as a tool, resource, point of contact, small rhyme, clue, or hint.

Teach Me

One way to verify that your know-how has become your learners' know-how-to is to get them to train someone else how to do it. Pretend that you are now the learner; ask them to take you through the same steps you used and transfer the know-how back to you. Act like a novice and only do as you are guided. Practice as they have you perform, but only do as well as they teach. Make the occasional error so your trainer has to provide feedback to get you back on track. Make the session dynamic. At the end, debrief and provide encouraging feedback. This is a great activity that builds competence and confidence. It is effective training for both of you. You could also have the learner train others while you observe and provide feedback.

Tried-and-True Techniques for Making Repetition and Practice Enjoyable and Effective

Here are four ways for making repetition and practice fun and effective, as well as examples of each technique in action. You can use any of them with individuals or teams to build speed, skill, and fluency, which is performance in a smooth, confident manner. Think about language—when you speak fluently, you say things without hesitation, with proper intonation or rhythm, and with little error. This happens because you've been practicing speaking your entire life. It's the same with playing a musical instrument, finding your way to a location, learning to type, or reciting a poem.

Make It a Rap

Repeat the words or steps. Give it a rhyme or a beat. This technique works well for remembering:

- Classes of hazardous goods
- Procedures for disassembling and assembling equipment

For example: To tie a tie, rap the following as you and the learner perform the actions:

1. Loop tie round neck, wide-side right and long.
2. Loop long round short, loose not strong.
3. Do it again 'cause wasn't that fun?
4. Pull long up behind short, then down front through loop.
5. Pull long down to end, in one fell swoop.
6. Tighten knot to even out short and long, then you're all done. Come on, man, wasn't that fun?

Ask Questions

Read or listen to content. Take notes. Then, convert each point to a question. Keep asking the questions until you get them all right. (Can be done in teams.) This technique works well for learning:

- Policies that must be internalized
- Product features and benefits
- Emergency shut-down procedures

For example, after taking a class on fire extinguishers and their uses, the learner uses their notes from the class to create a list questions:

- Which fire extinguisher is the only one to use for fires that start from combustible metals?
- Which is the best fire extinguisher to extinguish cooking fires?
- Is a Class C extinguisher good to use on electrical fires? Why or why not?

Then the occasional trainer and learner continuously review the questions and answer them until the learner can answer all questions correctly in random order.

Test Yourself

Make up test questions (or have learners make up test questions) for a body of material. Test until perfect.

Here are two examples of how you could use use this technique when studying two different subjects:

- A professional body of content for certification (such as law, accounting, or network engineering)
  - Are morals and ethics synonymous? Explain.
  - TCP versus UDP—which of these is a connectionless protocol?
  - What is the function of a proxy server?
- Security measures for various contexts (including physical, intellectual property, and antiterrorist)
  - What are RAMs?
  - Which type of security do alarms and sensors provide for?
  - Which type of security does encryption mainly apply to?

Use Diagrams or Other Visual Aids

Create a note-taking guide with a list of keywords that require explanations or elaborations, as well as unlabeled diagrams, matrixes, and flow diagrams with empty boxes. Fill them in as the content is provided and compare with the models. Study. Repeat until perfect.

This technique works well when learning:

- lots of processes and new vocabulary in a technical course
- body language in a course supplemented with illustrations of postures and meanings
- actions to put out different types of fires.

For example, if you wanted to remember the different parts of a neuron, which we discussed at the beginning of this chapter, you might use a diagram like the one on the next page. First, use a labeled image to identify all the parts, then cover the labels and practice your recall.

Use another blank version to see if you can successfully label all the parts without help.

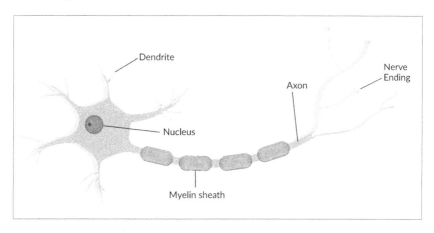

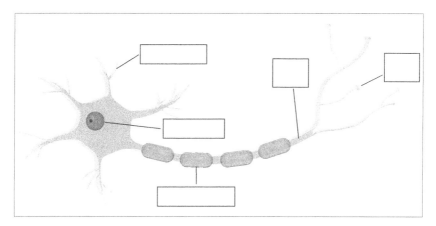

Summary

This chapter covered a lot of content. It began with the effect of practice on learning and long-term retention using a simple recall challenge activity to demonstrate how lots of practice, even early in life, produces speedy and accurate recall. We also discovered that learning is not easy, even though we are genetically programmed for it. We found that learning occurs when nerves and brain cells work together to form electrochemical connections within the neuron. We saw how focused, deliberate practice strengthens connections that generate learning speed, accuracy, and retention. We discussed stress, its triggers, and its positive and negative effects; we also discussed how, as an OT, you can reduce the negative effects of stress during the know-how transfer process. Finally, the chapter concluded with strategies for building learner confidence and success along with techniques for making repetition and practice fun and effective.

 REMEMBER THIS

Here are 10 statements drawn from the content of this chapter. Each contains a pair of optional choices (except for one that offers four choices) to help correctly complete each statement. Select your choices, then compare yours with ours.

1. Most people can complete the opening activity of this chapter in less than 30 seconds. This is possible because our responses are (*automatic/simply logical and easily reasoned out*).

2. We are programmed from birth to learn. This (*makes/doesn't necessarily make*) it easy for us to acquire new skills and knowledge.

3. A substance called myelin (*strengthens/weakens*) neural connections that (*allow learning to occur/prevent learning from occurring*).

4. Practice that repeats errors (*strengthens/weakens*) myelination, and thus (*speeds up/slows down*) the rate at which learning occurs.

5. The correct spelling of the word for a strong, regular, repeated pattern of movement or sound is (*rhythm/rhythem/rythem/rythm*).

6. Research indicates that continuous stress can (*adversely affect/ actually stimulate and enhance*) memory and learning over time.

7. The training context can play a (*major/minor*) role in triggering stress when a learner is acquiring new know-how-to.

8. Job aids and decision tables are (*distractions/useful tools*) for avoiding the consequences of errors.

9. (*Train–Rehearse–Restate/Teach–Prompt–Release*) is a strategy to help build learner confidence and success.

10. Using "rap" is (*a distracting/an enhancing*) technique that assists the recall of steps in a procedure.

And here's what we chose:

1. Most people can complete the opening activity of this chapter in less than 30 seconds. This is possible because our responses are *automatic*. As children, we were drilled in producing these responses until we got them perfect. Over the years, we have simply pulled them up automatically from memory whenever required. Highly practiced and perfected learning sticks to produce instant recall.

2. We are programmed from birth to learn. This *doesn't necessarily make* it easy for us to acquire new skills and knowledge. While we possess an innate aptitude to learn, we still must attend to what is important, attach it meaningfully to prior knowledge, sort through what goes with what, and create meaningful, usable, applicable capabilities. We are equipped to learn. But it is not easy.

3. A substance called myelin *strengthens* neural connections that *allow learning to occur*. Myelin is a chemical substance that wraps itself around an activated axon at a neuronal synapse to reinforce the connection. With repetition, the myelin thickens until the learning connection becomes automated.

4. Practice that repeats errors *weakens* myelination, and thus *slows down* the rate at which learning occurs.

5. The correct spelling of the word for a strong, regular, repeated pattern of movement or sound is *rhythm*. Rhythm makes your two hips move.

6. Research indicates that continuous stress can *adversely affect* memory and learning over time. Excessive cortisol can overexcite the brain, causing a decrease in rational thinking and acting, negative brain function, health issues, and other serious psychological and physical problems.

7. The training context can play a *major* role in triggering stress when a learner is acquiring new know-how-to. The physical and psychological characteristics of the environment—from unfamiliarity to overstimulation to cultural distractions—are

just some of the elements that can cause severe stress within the learner from uncertainties and insecurities to outright fears and inability to function.

8. Job aids and decision tables are *useful tools* for avoiding the consequences of errors. Practicing with these before introducing the learner to real-world cases can be a very effective way to anticipate and handle mistakes and mishaps.

9. *Teach – Prompt – Release* is a strategy to help build learner confidence and success.

10. Using "rap" is an *enhancing* technique that assists the recall of steps in a procedure. The rhythmic pattern facilitates memory.

Ready for the next chapter? It has a fun title and includes a lot of activities. It's filled with ideas for making your know-how transfer exciting for both you and your learners. Quick, turn the page!

7

TIPS, TRICKS, TOOLS, AND TIDBITS

CHAPTER HIGHLIGHTS:

- A toolbox of training-learning enhancements.
- Pull and push tips for enticing learning involvement.
- Techniques, tricks, and tools to spice up the know-how transfer process and improve stickiness.
- Tidbits for triggering insights and stirring the imagination.

This chapter focuses on usable ideas and techniques aimed at building engagement—which is the key to successful learning—and making transferred skills and knowledge stick. Our aim is to provide handy means and methods for keeping the OT hurtling along in a motivating, meaningful, and memorable manner. Each section offers a toolbox of training-learning enhancements aimed at stimulating know-how transfer.

Tips

It's important to grab the learner's attention right off the bat. One of the most effective ways of accomplishing this is by adopting a "pull" training approach. Think of a piece of string lying on a table. How can you make it move in the direction you want it to go? Do you push it or pull it? Pushing gets you nowhere—try it. Pulling, on the other hand, lets you rapidly move the string along.

We strongly encourage you, as an OT to draw (pull) from the learner as much as possible their needs, goals, questions, responses, actions, ideas, solutions, and inferences through careful set-ups and questions. Here are some examples:

- What do you want to accomplish?
- Wouldn't it be great if you could automatically find each item?
- What do you think this button does?
- Which of these choices makes better sense?
- If the avenue numbers are going up, how many blocks are there between Sixth Avenue and 10th Avenue?
- Select the tool you believe will work. What caused you to make this choice?
- Why didn't the screen show the item when you placed it in front of the scanner?

By *pulling* the answers or actions from the learner, you force active mental activity, which in turn sparks the learning. This works far better than telling, which is little more than pushing words and demonstrations at the learner.

The pull approach is also known as the Socratic method. Socrates, the Greek philosopher-teacher, frequently achieved learning results by drawing out from students correct responses they didn't know they possessed. In the *Meno*, one of Plato's *Dialogues*, Plato recounts how Socrates was able to get a randomly selected slave boy to use Pythagoras' Theorem to create a square exactly double the size of the original one, despite being completely ignorant of geometry. All through "pulling." Applying this method at each step of the Five-Step model results in rapid, continuous, and meaningful progress. The OT should constantly invite the learner to say and do more than the trainer.

Another helpful tip is to use analogies, metaphors, and rich examples to render abstract notions concrete. An analogy or comparison clarifies meaning and allows a concrete image to appear. Similarly, metaphors (*His steady stare was ice* or *Alice's long, flowing hair was an undulating, shining golden river*) and similes (*The embattled warrior fought like a ferocious tiger* or *Your explanation is as clear as mud*) create vivid images for the learner. Analogies, metaphors, similes, and image-rich examples help learners struggling to possess your know-how to "see" what you are attempting to make meaningful for them (for example, the day was rainy and cold so the child crept into the bed, crawled under the covers, and was soon *curled up as cozy and snug as a bug in a rug*).

Here are a few more tips to enrich your know-how to know-how-to sessions when working with learners:

- Instead of engaging with your learner face-to-face, shift your body so that you are interacting side-by-side. This way you can share the learner's visual perspective.
- Eliminate "I" and "I want you to. . . ." from your vocabulary when addressing the learner. Replace these words and phrases with "you" and "now you try this." Keep the spotlight on the learner and their activities.
- Focus any praise on task accomplishment, not on the person. (For example, instead of saying, "Wow! You did great," say, "Wow! You extracted the embryo from the egg perfectly by following the steps and manipulating your instrument at the appropriate angle. Perfect procedure. Perfect result.")

A final set of tips relates to the frequent use of feedback to your learner to shape how the learner performs. The list below lays out key dos and don'ts for providing feedback as well as an example.

- Never mix corrective with confirming feedback at the same time. This produces confusion. For example:
  - **Don't say:** You sliced the bagel into two equal halves. Good! But you sliced with the knife edge turned toward your body. That's dangerous! Always slice away from the body.
  - **Do:** Keep each action separate from one another. Focus on the corrective feedback first. Direct the learner to repeat the slicing action until they do it correctly. Then deal with the issue of the two equal halves.
- Express feedback through action or application statements. For example:
  - When you crossed the street, you turned your head left, then right, then left, and stepped off the sidewalk. But what is the rule in London? Yes! Look right, look left, look right, then step out if all clear. Repeat the rule. Let's practice again.
- Provide feedback not only after an attempt, but also just before the next one. For example:
  - Yesterday when you divided one half by one quarter you inverted the first fraction and multiplied by the second. The result was an error. What should you have done? Good. You corrected it. Remember this today when you try a new fraction division challenge.
- Include visual and other sensory information as well as verbal feedback. For example:
  - You placed the item in front of the scanner. Did you hear the scanner tone register the item? Did you see the item and price on the screen? Yes, to both questions! You got it right.
- Use the results of actions as feedback cues. For example:
  - You cleaned both broken ends and left no residue. Then you applied the glue to both broken surfaces separately and let

the surfaces dry for 15 minutes. Finally, you placed the broken ends together and steadily applied pressure for five minutes. Now, stand the bracket upright. Does it hold without wobble? Is the mend firm? Is there weakness at the joint? All tight? Great! Success!

Tricks and Tools

This section provides several tricks (useful tactics) as well as some handy training tools you can use to enliven your transfer of know-how. The purpose is to spice up learning and increase long-term retention, also known as stickiness.

A Picture Is Worth 1,000 Words

Words often get in the way and clutter the mind. A visual representation such as a photo of an event,

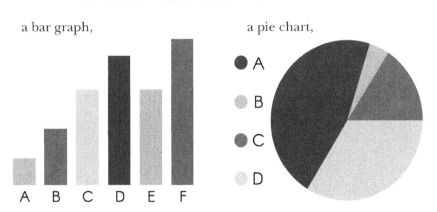

a bar graph,   a pie chart,

or a simple line drawing,

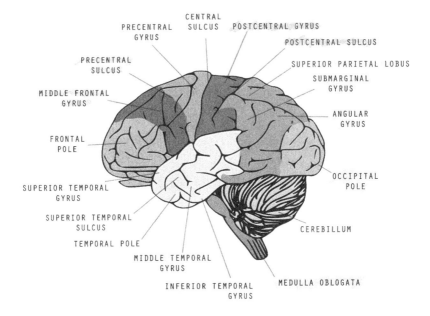

more powerfully illustrates the point than words ever will.

Words Are Powerful Too

Conversely, a word or two can sometimes convey the meaning more powerfully than a picture. This is especially true when expressing:

- emotional or psychological states (paranoia or stress)
- precise measures (3.4 grams, 26.2 miles or an IQ of 140)
- abstract notions (intelligence or insomnia).

Use the Senses

Employ real or simulated objects and models to inject multisensory dimensions into the training-learning process, for example:

- smell in the case of spices
- taste to discern differences in wine varietals
- vision to choose between two types of pliers
- hearing to determine if it's a violin or a viola
- sensory immersion to experience the loss of equilibrium or the sense of constriction from a blood pressure monitoring device

Job Aids Rule

Whenever possible, create and apply job aids to produce successful performance. In fact, well-constructed job aids can often replace training. Successful job aid use produces instant performance results. (For example, use a train timetable rather than show how to obtain information about train arrivals and departures. The only training required would be on how to use the job aid if it is not intuitive.)

Tidbits

This final section closes the chapter with examples of "aha!" learning that trigger instant insights and increase the probability of long-term retention. We occasionally like to include flights of fantasy and weirdness to add zest to our transfer activities. When done right, even simple activities can lead to complex reflections. The key point is that once the light bulb turns on and the learner "gets it," it sticks.

Get Weird

Is your learner dealing with a difficult co-worker or are you dealing with a difficult learner? You may be focusing all your energy on how much you want to get away from this obnoxious person. STOP! Instead, imagine being that horrid person. What would it be like to live inside their body? And think about this: Eventually, you can get away from that individual. They can't get away from themselves . . . ever! That person is stuck with their obnoxiousness. Are you starting to feel sadness and empathy for them? As you reflect on how fortunate you are, your pain will soon go away! What a relief! What an aha!

Here's a fun example of using a fantastical scenario to develop practical know-how survival skills. Did you know that the US military planned and executed a large-scale simulated training attack on Paradise Point Resort, a 44-acre island off the coast of San Diego, California?[7] The attackers were zombies. This is no joke! The entire fantasy invasion—involving more than 1,000 military personnel, Hollywood-style sets, and real equipment—was aimed at fostering learning on how to deal with an unlikely event filled with a host of unpredictable behaviors. While this may seem strange at first, many "serious" professionals (including businesses, policy planners, and engineers) employ fantasy to create immersive training environments for individuals to learn and adapt to unexpected conditions. The fantasy elements can increase focus and motivation. Through a simulated zombie attack, you can create a training scenario that requires the learner to practice skills with increasing speed and dexterity, make decisions, adapt to new conditions, and rework plans to meet shifting, escalating challenges. But it is more enjoyable and thus "stickier" than simply recreating a work crisis. Even visits to made-up locations can become vehicles for discovery, map reading, or calculation of resource requirements.[8]

Create a Mental Picture

Mentally imagining or creating a visual of how something looks can be a powerful means for rendering concrete what might remain abstract for learners.

We know that 3D vision can be a difficult concept for anyone to comprehend, especially a child. Here is a simple exercise kids can do to see how it works in real life. Mark a small X on one side of their right forefinger, at about the middle of the nail. Have them point their forefinger toward the tip of their nose, starting about a foot out. Then have them slowly move their finger toward their nose. Ask them to call out when the X disappears, and explain that it's because they can no longer focus both of their eyes to see both sides of their finger. Tell them to continue advancing their finger until they touch their nose. At this point, they can no longer see depth. Have them count the number of fingers they see. (Three.) They have "lost a finger!" As they slowly pull back their finger, their 3D vision begins to return. Discuss. It's dramatic, and this lesson will stay with the children for a long time.

In addition, objectively viewing what reality is or can be can alter your perception of what is going on. We've shared a personal example of this in our journal entry on the next page.

From Our Personal Journal

When we got married, one of the many adjustments we had to make was to our eating behaviors. Erica was raised in the United States and was used to desserts, especially ice cream. Harold, raised on French cuisine, naturally incorporated wine, bread, and cheese into his dinners. Unfortunately, only a few months after combining these taste preferences, we realized that we'd both gained about 10 pounds each!

Immediate corrective action was required. We began counting our calories and quickly discovered the necessity of applying portion control. We hadn't been paying attention to how much we were consuming. We found, for example, wine can be consumed in highly variable quantities, which can easily be masked by the size and shape of the wine glass.

So, we began by conjuring up the image of how we poured and sipped our wines. Then, we filled a measuring cup with five ounces of water and poured a series of five-ounce portions into the different wine glasses we owned. When we lined the glasses up in a row the result was astounding! The levels of liquid in each glass were markedly different.

Our next experiment was to pour our regular amounts of wine into each glass. When we measured the contents by pouring each back into a measuring cup, we discovered that we had been consuming between 4.0 and 6.5 ounces per glass, depending on the wine glass. And it was usually toward the upper end of the scale!

We also found that a scoop of ice cream can be equally deceiving, depending on the size of scoop and bowl. What we thought was a half-cup portion often turned out to be a full cup (equaling two servings and twice the calories!)

We truly learned the value of translating what we imagined to reality! Seeing these authentic measures radically altered our perceptions, behaviors, and, thankfully, our waistlines.

Whatever you do as an OT, capturing and maintaining your learner's attention is a necessity and constant challenge. The more you engage the learner, the more effective the know-how transfer. We strongly advocate a "love 'em or lose 'em" approach to training (which is also the title of a highly successful book by author and workplace performance consultant Beverly Kaye). As an OT, you should communicate your joy into each training-learning encounter. Inject imagination into all your know-how transfer efforts and release your creativity by applying what you've learned here. Then strike out beyond!

 ## REMEMBER THIS

In this chapter, we inundated you with ideas for enhancing the appeal of your occasional training. Now let's see if you remember them. Read the statements below and choose your preferred option within the parentheses. Then compare your choices with ours.

1. A pull training approach (*draws from/presses into*) the learner the answers, questions, actions, solutions, and inferences.

2. (*Analogies, similes, and metaphors/Detailed explanations*) are effective means for rendering abstract notions concrete.

3. Image-rich examples (*help learners see what the OT is attempting to make meaningful to them/just add words to an explanation and generally confuse learners*).

4. Sitting (*side-by-side/face-to-face*) with your learner during know-how transfer sessions changes the traditional teacher-student setup in training.

5. Focus praise on the (*person rather than task accomplishment/task accomplishment rather than the person*) when providing confirming feedback to a learner.

6. It (*is/is not*) a good idea to review corrective feedback from a previous trial with the learner prior to making a new attempt.

7. A picture can often replace many words (*and a single word or sentence can be more effective than a picture/but a single word or sentence can never replace a picture*).

8. Using integrated stimulation from a variety of senses simultaneously generally results in (*more authentic learning/learning confusion*).

9. Fantasy storylines and scenarios (*can spice up serious learning and increase the sense of authenticity of a situation/distracts from serious learning and obscures authenticity*).

Now for our responses and comments.

1. A pull training approach *draws from* the learner's answers, questions, actions, solutions, and inferences. Pull implies drawing forth. As the string analogy suggests, when you pull a string, it moves more rapidly and efficiently than when you try to push it.

2. *Analogies, similes, and metaphors* are effective means for rendering abstract notions concrete. They build a bridge between the known and the unknown (for example, *the child's face beamed like the shining sun*). This creates a powerful means for initiating instant comprehension by connecting something new with something familiar. Detailed explanation, on the other hand, is often verbose, overwhelming, and even tedious.

3. Image-rich examples *help learners see what the OT is attempting to make meaningful to them.* If the image rich examples connect with what the learner has already experienced, meaningfulness emerges rapidly. The example of a customer being received at a restaurant the same way they would welcome a dear relative into their home quickly communicates how the restaurant owner expects his employees to greet guests.

4. Sitting *side-by-side* with your learner during know-how transfer sessions changes the traditional teacher-student setup in training. Being at the learner's side, at the same level and viewing things from their perspective, changes the dynamic of the trainer-learner interaction.

5. Focus praise on *task accomplishment rather than the person* when providing confirming feedback to a learner. The research strongly suggests that feedback directed toward a person can have less predictable results than if it's directed to the task accomplishment and no personal element is involved. This removes any chance of implied judgment of the individual receiving the feedback.

6. It *is* a good idea to review corrective feedback from a previous trial with the learner prior to making a new attempt. Reminding the learner of a prior attempt that was successful and of what made it so increases the probability of success this time around.

7. Pictures can often replace many words *and a single word or sentence can be more effective than a picture.* A simple sentence, such as "His very nature screamed 'rabid hatred,'" conveys a great deal of meaning. A single picture might not generate such a powerful image. Both pictures and words have their places apart and together.

8. Using coordinated stimulation from a variety of senses simultaneously generally results in *more authentic learning.* Imagine using loud motor noises, heavy pressure against the chest, and a strong, jerking movement to provide a sense of rapid acceleration. Even touching and viewing a piece of equipment creates more complete meaning during learning, especially when the content is novel or unfamiliar.

9. Fantasy storylines and scenarios *can spice up serious learning and increase the sense of authenticity of a situation.* When a sense of strangeness, time criticality, and elements of unfamiliarity are injected into a scenario in a believable way, heart rate, focus, respiration, and adrenaline are all affected. This increases believability and creates a heightened sense of authenticity in learning.

We had fun writing this chapter. Its content is like a spice rack. Incorporate these ideas into your activities as appropriate to enhance them and create unique flavors.

Now, take a well-deserved break. You earned it!

Building Confidence, Not Just Competence

CHAPTER HIGHLIGHTS:
- Competence: one word, many dimensions.
- The difference between skill and competency.
- The critical role of confidence in learning and performance.
- Confidence: too much, too little, or just right?

This chapter focuses on a very important but often insufficiently addressed factor that plays a huge role in how effectively a new learner applies know-how-to in the real world. Without enough confidence, a novice may experience uncertainty with new know-how, leading to an inability to apply what they have learned. Let's examine the ingredients that go into the application of capability to perform, especially of anything new:

- **Skill** is the ability to do something. The skilled person owns this skill, which can take many forms:
  - physical (dance the tango, hit a target using a bow and arrow, or type 100 words a minute)
  - verbal (recite a lengthy poem, spell complicated words, or accurately describe the actions and recite players' names during a fast-moving soccer match)
  - analytical (diagnose a noisy car engine, solve a mathematical problem, select the best strategy for achieving a goal)
  - artistic (walk a tightrope, sing an operatic aria, or paint a lush landscape).
- **Competency** is an ability that is required for a job, such as suturing a wound, baking a sourdough baguette, or providing accurate and complete directions to a tourist. You always begin with the job to define required competencies. You assess people to identify their relevant skills. You then seek to match a person's skills with job competency requirements. If you cannot perfectly match these, you find those with similar skill sets and suitable characteristics, and then train them to meet the needed competency standards.
- **Performance** is the outcome of doing a task that leads to an accomplishment. (For example, slicing a bagel = doing. Slicing a bagel into two equal halves with smooth surfaces and no injuries = performance.) A person needs competency to perform. In the know-how transfer process, acquisition of performance capability is targeted, and the novice learner becomes equipped to perform.
- **Motivation** is a person's internal state, which drives them to engage, act, and persist at doing something. (For example, run

a marathon, help a person in trouble, memorize the elements of the periodic table, or convert a customer service request into a successful add-on sale.) Without motivation, while know-how transfer may be present, it is inert because the learner lacks the propelling motivational component to push for application of what they have acquired.

The OT must clearly and forcefully communicate several things during the know-how transfer process:

- The *value* of what the learner is acquiring—for them most of all, as well as others including customers, employers, or co-workers. The OT must present a clear value proposition for the learner applying the new know-how-to and also for others who will benefit from the learning.
- *Learner confidence* creates a strong sense of self-efficacy or can-do during the knowledge transfer process. The learner should think, "This is something I can perform."
- *Positive mood* or outlook on the usefulness or appropriateness of applying the new know-how-to.

The OT is key to reinforcing the value of what is being learned, building learner confidence that they "can do this" and creating a positive mood or good feeling about applying the acquired know-how-to and achieving the outcome.

The obvious challenge for the OT is to build talk-about or do competencies. Talk-about competencies are declarative (name, list, describe, recount or explain) versus do competencies, which are procedural (solve, select, or execute tasks).

And the OT also needs to build the right level of confidence while producing competence. Remember these two important rules about learner confidence:

- If learners become overconfident, they tend to become neglectful and cocky and make unnecessary mistakes. Accidents and errors can ensue. Overconfident thoughts include "this is easy; no problem; or piece of cake."

- If learners don't feel confident, they tend to get flustered and clumsy, as well as make unnecessary errors or refuse to try. They freeze or offer excuses and avoid effort. Lack of confidence causes thoughts like, "this is too hard; I will probably make a mistake; there's too much danger; or I'll look foolish trying."

Either case produces a negative effect on learner performance.

Balance is the name of the game. It'll help your learner achieve the right level of confidence during the know-how to know-how-to transfer process.

From Our Journal

We once helped a telephone company's customer service agents transform from simply "servicing" customers to becoming promoters and sellers of the company's additional products, services, and programs. Before we came in, the customer service agent would help customers who called in with a service request or billing issue by simply making any suitable adjustments.

The company believed that these moments would serve as great opportunities to offer additional products, services, and programs as appropriate. The goal was to improve agent communication and sales capabilities as well as potentially save customers money while growing sales revenues for the company—an apparent win-win for all. However, because the agents had never played the role of salesperson, this created a cultural shock, resulting in high levels of discomfort and a sense of "This is not who I am!" and "I provide service; I don't sell."

The company asked personnel who had similar customer service backgrounds and sales experience to serve as OTs. They would conduct individual and small group sessions to train and coach the agents in the new sales know-how. While the transfer sessions went relatively smoothly, attempts by learners to apply their new know-how-to capabilities were filled with hesitation, fear, awkwardness, and a reluctance to apply the new skills with customers. This adversely affected the timeline for the agent conversion process.

However, we worked with the company to create carefully guided practice and celebrate small successes. Trainee confidence soon began to build along with newly acquired competencies. The agents began to view many of their new job requirements as being helpful for customers. They also gained a broader understanding of what their company offered beyond what they had understood before.

Tips for Building Appropriate Know-How Transfer Confidence

Let's look at a few useful tips for the OT:

- Demonstrate in word and deed that you are entirely confident the learner can do it. Don't present a false sense of bravado. Explain how others have done it. If necessary, provide credible examples, which allow the learner to see that success is achievable.
- Build a sense of security. State that you are there to observe and support the learner's practice with guidance and helpful hints. Also, remind them of available follow-up support or offer readily accessible resources once the know-how training is done. Build confidence through support availability.
- Reinforce or reward all novice learner application success. This encourages them to try out activities and increases their motivation.
- If the learner experiences difficulties during application, break down the know-how transfer process into smaller, simpler chunks and reward the success of each chunk. Piece them together slowly and meaningfully.
- Use examples along the way to make any abstract notions seem more concrete. This helps the learner better visualize what is going on.
- Continually emphasize the value of know-how transfer. Point out any benefits for the learner and as many other people as possible.
- Demonstrate your pride in the learner's accomplishments.

As for dampening overconfidence:

- Quickly note errors of speed, accuracy, missed steps, or outward signs of carelessness. Reinforce successes but remember to caution against too much self-assurance. By monitoring any unnecessary glitches, the learner learns to increase vigilance and reduce error rates.

- Provide self-checklists with questions such as, "Did you do. . . ?" or items such as, "List the steps you took." When the learner reflects on what they did, it strengthens appropriate practice.

- If you are working with more than one learner, have them observe each other to provide and receive feedback. This helps reinforce best practices.

- Stress the importance of care and accuracy rather than speed to increase competence.

- Have the learner do things more than once if overconfidence manifests itself; make sure to point out the consequences and dangers of feeling too secure.

Confidence is as critical to know-how transfer as competence, so maintaining the confidence balance is essential for the OT's success. Let's quickly review with our end-of-chapter Remember This questions.

 REMEMBER THIS

Select the most appropriate option for each statement.

1. In know-how transfer, confidence on the part of the learner is (*as important as/relatively important compared with*) competence.

2. Lack of confidence in successfully applying new know-how-to is (*an uncommon/a common*) experience in knowledge transfer efforts.

3. Competencies are specified in terms of (*external requirements derived from a task or job analysis/demonstrated capabilities derived from individual assessments*).

4. The drive within us to engage, act, and persist at a task is called (*incentive/motivation*).

5. As an OT, demonstrate that you are (*entirely/moderately*) confident the novice learner can do the task.

And now for our responses and remarks.

1. In know-how transfer, confidence on the part of the learner is *as important as* competence. Capability to perform is a necessary but insufficient condition for transfer to occur. The learner must possess ample confidence to engage, apply, and persist in the transfer process.

2. Lack of confidence to successfully apply new know-how-to is *a common* experience in knowledge transfer efforts.

3. Competencies are specified in terms of *external requirements derived from a task or job analysis*. We first analyze a task or job to determine the competencies required to achieve success. This is external to people. Then we recruit and assess individuals to measure how well the skills they possess match up with the competency requirements.

4. The drive within us to engage, act, and persist at a task is called *motivation*. Incentives can be used to stimulate motivation; for example, if you offer $10 to wash the dishes it motivates your teenager to engage, wash the dishes, and persist through to the drying and stacking the dishes.

5. As an OT, demonstrate that you are *entirely* confident the novice learner can do it. The OT must show complete confidence the learner can perform.

This chapter focused on the importance of confidence and the roles OTs play in fostering the required confidence in the appropriate doses. The importance of learner confidence cannot be overstated. Think back to the customer service reps in our journal example who eventually became successful salespeople by solving customer problems and meeting needs. The customers, the company, and the agents benefited from the transformation. A win-win-win! Kudos to the OTs!

9

Support! Support! Support!

Just as the Beatles song "HELP!" laments, we often need "somebody, not just anybody," even if we previously felt self-assured. One of the biggest failures of any type of training stems from releasing learners into the world to perform too quickly. Most workplace, educational, and informal training severs the trainer-learner connection too abruptly once the session is over. Just because the trainees have supposedly demonstrated that they can do it or passed some sort of test doesn't mean they're ready to go solo.[9]

Left alone, especially if there is a time gap between the training experience and real-life application, human tendencies toward forgetfulness, uncertainty, lack of practice, or new environments all rear their ugly heads. The result? "Help! I can no longer do it." This is especially true when the training source was an OT with little or no infrastructure or support ties to the learner.

Let's examine a few examples:

- Martha found herself doing well at Bargain City's self-checkout counter. Even with a couple glitches, she figured out how to properly weigh various fruits and vegetables. However, when she shopped at Melville's Market, she became confused because the self-checkout system was a bit different. She became disoriented and unable to perform.

- Despite reviewing with the hotel concierge how to find their way to the theater in Manhattan, the Khans somehow got lost. Did they make a wrong turn? Had they misread a street sign? (Was it 12th Street or Avenue? Did they turn on 23rd Street West or East?)

- Gregoire practiced entering data during the know-how transfer session. He took notes and successfully repeated the steps under the eye of the OT. However, when he tried to replicate his new know-how-to back at his desk, he encountered repeated error messages. It had looked easy. He had been confident in his ability to do it during the session. But now he felt lost.

- Jane's best friend taught her how to waltz. They had practiced a lot and got feedback on several different dances. Jane was into it. However, on her first outing with a new partner, she became awkward and could not keep up. What an embarrassment!

What went wrong? In all these cases, new circumstances led to mishaps, disorientation, initial error, loss of confidence (most likely), and an inability to continue. Let's look at how some form of support might have helped in each situation.

- **The self-checkout issue.** Anticipating that variations in checkout systems will occur, the OT must inform the learner that there are many different self-checkout systems and allude to variations during training. If possible, simulate "what if" situations and practice them. While we can't foresee all variations, we can practice questions to ask when we run into issues. During the training, the OT can have the novice observe others doing their checkout and practice asking other shoppers to explain what they did. Train for self-reliance. Guide them to seek help within a new store to adapt to changes. Give them a small card with notes on it for "What to do when you get stuck," with tips like, "If this happens, do this or ask this."

- **Getting lost in Manhattan.** The OT should anticipate how a person might go astray when following directions to a venue and note those on a map. Ask the person to recite back how they will proceed and what to watch for. Provide feedback as appropriate. Give novices a tool of some sort to which they can refer as well as simple questions to ask locals if they get lost. Provide a hotel referral number or phone app to help get them back on track.

- **Can't replicate new know-how-to on the job.** Sometimes a new environment or piece of equipment will change how things work. Discuss these differences during the know-how transfer session to anticipate what might go wrong. The OT should demonstrate and problem solve with the learner. Prepare the novice to troubleshoot, ask fellow workers questions, and look up problem-solving resources. Provide a number they can call for help or a website to access solutions.

- **So you think you can dance?** We once took dance lessons. Neither of us is naturally nimble, but we had a teacher who was wonderful. It was awkward and painful, but we managed to eventually get it. Great feeling! That is until we went to a real dance. The floor, the lighting, the tempo, and the ambiance were all different from the training setting. What could the OT have done to help us better prepare for the highly anticipated dance?

- Practice with other people.
- Go to at least one intermediary venue that was less threatening than a real-world, full-dress dance environment to practice.
- Provide a job aid and advice about what to practice and how to get ready for the real-world dance scene.
- Give tips on practicing at home and with different pieces of music.
- Schedule multiple sessions before moving out of the training environment.

The success of the know-how transfer depends a lot on the entry-level of the novice learner. If the gap between this initial level and what is being transferred is large, the transfer must take place in small steps. If this is true, if the learner's confidence level is low, or if there are many variations in application, you must factor this into how you conduct yourself as an OT.

As another Beatles song emphasizes, most people require "a little help from a friend."

Remedies for Providing Support Once the Know-How Training Has Ended

When you are in an occasional training situation, it is likely to be informal or even impromptu, which means there won't be any professionally prepared materials for learners. Instead, you'll need to rely on what is available or can be repurposed as a training aid. What follows is a list of frequently used support methods and materials that OTs can employ.

Over Practice

In an earlier chapter, we mentioned that deliberate practice—repetition to strengthen learning with feedback focused on improvement—results in greater accuracy, increased speed of accomplishment, decreased effort, and performance fluency and efficiency. Like a hockey player repeatedly shooting goals from different angles, this continuous over practicing produces long-lasting, post-training success. It causes retention to become hardwired into the learner's repertoire.

Memory Aids

If you can't hardwire know-how transfer into the brain, the next-best approach is to provide memory aids and help the user practice using these tools. A few examples of mnemonic devices include:

- NEWS (north, east, west, south) for the cardinal points of a compass.
- Every good boy deserves fun (E, G, B, D, F) to name the lines of the treble clef and FACE for the spaces between the lines.
- TWEEK is a mnemonic we personally use. It stands for telephone, wallet, eyes (eyeglasses), ears (hearing aids), and keys. Harold uses TWEEK to verify he has all five items with him before leaving the house or office. Without TWEEKing, he often forgets something.

Other memory aids include sticky notes, calendars (paper or electronic), to-do lists, alarms, weekly pill boxes for medications, and rhymes (I before E except after C or when sounded like A as in neighbor and weigh, and weird is just weird, so what can I say?)

Job Aids

These are external memory triggers. To obtain instant performance success, all you need do is learn how to use them. Examples of job aids include:

- GPS systems help you figure out how to get places. Simply enter the start and destination points in Google Maps to see directions, a map, an itinerary, and the distance as well as the time it takes to arrive by foot, bike, car, or public transportation. You can even receive step-by-step audio guidance by pressing START.
- Calculators can perform any calculation and instantaneously provide a perfectly accurate response.
- Online recipes, which may even include videos, show you how to bake a cherry pie or cook a pot roast.

- Color charts can help when dealing with colors. You may need to match hydraulic fluid in a transparent tube to determine viscosity or determine if seeing blue text in a chart is a good or bad sign.
- YouTube is a good source for finding videos that walk you through processes step-by-step. You can find anything from how to safely change a tire to how to chop down a tree.
- Recorded audio tours guide you on scenic walks around the Montmartre in Paris or provide more information as you look at exhibits in a museum.

In all instances, the OT's job is no longer to facilitate know-how transfer of the actual task, but to ensure you know how to use the job aid or system to find your way in your new job. It's a huge difference! You're using the same know-how transfer principles but for a much less complex task. The danger comes when you simply refer the learner to the job aid without ensuring they can use it effectively.

Resource Materials

Maps, guidebooks, catalogs, pamphlets, photos (on paper or online), manuals, directories, kiosks, standard operating procedures materials—the list of potential resources is endless. With some careful planning and researching, OTs can uncover a great deal of available resources, often in advance, to facilitate know-how transfer.

Helplines

The internet is probably the best place to find a helpline. However, internal helplines—those within organizations or industries and public/governmental agencies—are more available than you might realize.

Reference Guides

Help learners perform by giving them extra assistance in the form of specialized dictionaries, atlases, grammar books, visual dictionaries, thesauruses, technical reference manuals, star charts, and mortgage rate calculators. The OT and the internet are excellent starter sources for hunting these down. Make sure to build the means for finding and using appropriate reference guides into the know-how transfer process.

As you can see, resources for post know-how transfer support are readily available! You just have to know where to look. To conclude this section, here are a few more resources to add to your growing list:

- Provide names, email addresses, and phone numbers learners can turn to when they forget. For example, Joe in the machine shop; the shift supervisor; Auntie Sophie, who baked Granny's cherry pie many times.
- Online resources, such as YouTube, provide an amazing resource for how to do almost anything. Use the search function on any computer browser to find online helplines.
- Local groups are also excellent resources. For example, hobby groups to help with model train assembly or local agencies such as classic car clubs for restoration tips.
- Physical materials, such as maps, posters, and publication lists, are available at local historical societies, libraries, and public places.

From Our Journal

We recently acquired a new puppy, a beautiful Havanese we named Buttercup. Unfortunately, although we'd been adoptive puppy parents many years before, our initial delight soon turned to feelings of concern, such as giving oral medications, housebreaking, and not jumping on people. Informal OTs tried to help us, including our veterinarian, pet store personnel, and other dog owners. We were also astonished by how many helplines we had available to access—from pet food companies, breeder associations, and the American Kennel Club to pet store chains, the ASPCA, dog shelters, and dog lover communities. We found a vast array of knowledgeable people online who were ready to share their experiences and resources with anyone seeking help.

Using Support Materials

Let's carry out a simple exercise. Review all of the support methods and resources in this chapter and think about how they could be used in the know-how transfer sessions listed in the table below. We suggest you start with three scenarios and decide which three methods or resources you would recommend for know-how-to support post-training. To get you started, we did the exercise too! We had fun hunting around and testing our findings, which are entered in the table. We challenge you to come up with ones we have not listed. Like us, you will probably discover that limiting yourself to only three is a challenge.

WHAT CAN I USE FOR POST-TRAINING SUPPORT?

Transfer Session	Our Suggestions for Post-Training Support
Play chess (beginner)	• Over or deliberate practice • Illustrated memory aids (to show moves) • Electronic chessboards with increasingly difficult play levels and chess problems
Bake a Lasagna	• Recipes and cookbooks • Internet videos (How to. . . .) • Friends and neighbors who cook or bake Italian food
Solve crossword puzzles	• Internet (Google) • Good crossword puzzle dictionaries • Crossword communities and clubs (local or online)
Pass a volleyball to a teammate for a perfect set-up	• Over or deliberate practice • Fellow and advanced players • Volleyball clubs
Bathe a puppy	• Pet store or groomer • Veterinarian • Internet video
Select the right car for you and whether to buy, finance, or lease	• Online car-buyer guides and tools (such as Edmunds) • Blue Book • Car magazines, articles, and reviews
Set up and maintain a ledger	• Business, bookkeeper, and accountant friends • Online tutorials, guides, tools, and examples • How-to books
Write your own legal will	• Paper or online job aids, guides, forms, and tools • AARP • For-hire online or local consultants (to guide or provide models)

| Knowledgeably attend an opera | • Opera clubs
• People who regularly attend operas
• Books and internet sites on how to "get into opera" |
| Paint the interior of your house | • Paint stores
• Paint company videos, brochures, and charts
• A friendly neighborhood handyman |

We were overwhelmed with the number of support ideas and resources for every scenario! We hope you got a lot out of this exercise. Bear in mind that this treasure trove is as valuable to the OT as the novice learner.

We conclude this chapter with an effective support cue: Letting your learner know that post-training help is readily available, as well as where to obtain it, reassures novices who are ready to apply their know-how-to. Give them a way to report back on their first independent success effort. This reassures them and gives you a great pat on the back—one you richly deserve.

 REMEMBER THIS

Read each statement below and select the option that best fits. Then compare your choices with ours.

1. Once your learner has demonstrated the ability to perform by the end of the know-how transfer training session and can "do it," you (*can rest assured/may still have lingering doubts*) that they will be successful in their real-world know-how-to application.

2. In transferring know-how, simulating variations in application situations and practicing posing questions to people who appear to know how to perform is a (*great/confusing*) way to prepare novice learners for real-world success.

3. (*An excellent/a dangerous*) way to transfer know-how is to focus on confusing steps or ambiguous points during training to anticipate or avoid errors when applying new know-how-to.

4. Prior to the big dance, the OT might provide the dance novice (*practice in varied rehearsal environments with several different partners/ diagrams of dance steps to study and repeat alone at home*) to support acquisition of their new dancing know-how-to.

5. The larger the gap between the novice's current knowledge and expected know-how-to exit level, the (*larger/smaller*) the individual knowledge chunks the OT must transfer during training.

6. Over practice through deliberate repetition with feedback, highly focused on continuous improvement (*increases/does not increase*) the probability of know-how transfer success.

7. Know-how transfer support resources are (*not easily/readily*) available for most tasks.

And here, with comments, are our selections.

1. Once your learner has demonstrated the ability to perform by the end of the know-how transfer training session and can "do it," you *may still have lingering doubts* that they will succeed in their know-how-to application in the real world. We already referenced the Beatles about how we all need some help, even if we were previously self-assured. Perhaps we may have appeared to overemphasize the value of support while the training is still in progress and afterward. However, too much training—know-how transfer—gets lost due to lack of support. Believe it!

2. In transferring know-how, simulating variations in application situations and practicing posing questions to people who appear to know how to perform is *a great* way to prepare novice learners for real-world success. The more prepared the learner, the more effective the result. Once the novice is out there trying out their new know-how-to, asking for assistance from knowledgeable others is a useful skill for successful performance.

3. An *excellent* way to transfer know-how is to focus on confusing steps or ambiguous points during training to anticipate or avoid errors when applying new know-how-to.

4. Prior to the big dance, the OT might provide the dance novice *practice in varied rehearsal environments with several different partners* to support acquisition of their new dancing know-how-to.

5. The larger the gap between the novice's current knowledge and the expected know-how-to exit level, the *smaller* the individual knowledge chunks the OT must transfer during training. If the

gap is big, break down transfer learning into small, meaningful chunks and ensure mastery of each one. Rehearse putting them all together meaningfully!

6. Over practice through deliberate repetition with feedback, highly focused on continuous improvement *increases* the probability of know-how transfer success. Over practice of this nature leads to *automaticity*, a psychological term that means the learning has become automated. Like riding a bicycle, it sticks for a long time.

7. Know-how transfer support resources are *readily* available for most tasks. Once the OT knows what the know-how transfer requirement is, as this chapter has demonstrated, resources and support possibilities abound. The OT just needs to research and prep with imagination.

By now, you have accumulated a great deal of know-how about occasional training. This book is intended to act as a support resource once you have completed it. Every chapter is full of tips, tools, and guidance on how to put into practice what we have shared in our attempt to make our know-how your know-how-to. However, there are still a few more useful things to squeeze in on occasional training. Please stick with us a bit more—we don't want to let you go just yet. Chapter 10 focuses on the question, "Did they get it?" As an OT, you work hard to make sure you successfully transfer your knowledge. Are you sure the learners can perform? Let's turn the page to find out.

10

The Proof of the Pudding

CHAPTER HIGHLIGHTS:

- So, did transfer take place? There's only one way to know.
- In informal and occasional settings, is testing too intimidating? Is it even necessary?
- Testing can be fun!
- Testing: A wonderful way to provide opportunities for successful performance.
- If the learner didn't demonstrably learn, then the trainer didn't train successfully.

The old English expression "The proof of the pudding is in the eating" means you can only judge what has been done through the experienced or demonstrated result.[10] This is 100 percent true in the case of training and know-how transfer. What the OT does—all the words and activities delivered—comes down to a test or through concrete proof: Can the learner perform? Did know-how transfer take place in a verifiable manner? This chapter stresses that whatever effort you, as an OT, expend from sharing your know-how amounts to little if, for example, your roommate can't remember how to make a bed with hospital corners like you showed her or your colleague fails to retrieve accidentally deleted data. In short, OT success is contingent on learner success.

So, does this mean that to be successful as an OT, you *must* test? Sounds harsh, right? Especially if you are simply helping a person find the restroom. Let us probe a bit. Is it possible that testing is too scary or stressful or that it's overkill, particularly in informal learning settings? Do we want to frighten our learners? Most people do not really like being tested, because that word generally makes you feel like you are being weighed and measured to determine if you are good enough. This is an aberration. Testing is all about outcome. It is the means by which we check whether a desired end has been attained in a prespecified way—we *test* the water to see if it is the right temperature. *It is not about the value of a person but the attainment of an accomplishment.*

The great news about tests in a learning environment is that they can certify whether what is desired has been achieved. If you are supposed to get from here to there and demonstrate that you can, then, bravo, you have passed the test! Testing is great way to let learners know they are successful. In this context, the OT must not only test (that is, require demonstration of performance in a non-threatening way) but also provide positive (but also constructive) feedback on the result, either confirming or correcting with guidance to improve the outcome.

Tests do not have to be hard, tricky, or frightening. For learning purposes, an OT should set things up in such a way that the learner is virtually guaranteed success.

About the Word "Test"

A test does not have to look like a test; you don't even have to call it a test! For example, if a friend asks you how to create a contact in her smartphone's address book, how might you test to verify if the know-how you provided was successfully transferred? Here are some possibilities:

- Have the friend instruct you on how to do it on your phone.
- Have the friend create another new contact on her own phone.
- Have the friend create a job aid or simple set of directions that another person can apply to add a new contact on their own phone.

All of these are ways of verifying the know-how transfer. Whichever option you choose, the important point is to ensure performance capability before releasing your learner. Use any words that fit, such as, "Let's see if you got it" or "Play it back to me" or even "Now you teach me how to do it." Let's examine an actual case to see how this can work in the real world.

GERTRUDE'S WISH: BECOME A MAH JONGG PLAYER

Gertrude had been dying to join her friends when they played Mah Jongg. The game uses plastic or ivory tiles covered with Chinese symbols and employs a vocabulary that is unlike anything she had ever encountered. It uses a unique set of rules, which include a winning formula that changes annually (at least in the American version). The playing procedures are also somewhat arcane. But her friends love it, and she would really like to be part of their world.

Almost all "Mahj" trainers are OTs, and the transfer of Mahj know-how can be tricky. Entry level prior knowledge on the part of new learners is generally limited. So how did Gertrude proceed? She turned to her cousin, Winona, who had played for years.

A retired bookkeeper, Winona was an experienced player, but she'd never taught anyone to play Mah Jongg before. To prepare for the task, she created a list of know-how transfer lessons. Each lesson had an objective for Gertrude to master:

- ❑ State the objective of Mah Jongg.
- ❑ Identify each component of the game.
- ❑ Name each of the 152 tiles and pronounce their names accurately.
- ❑ Set up a game so it's ready to play.
- ❑ Execute the move known as the Charleston.
- ❑ Successfully play a practice game.

For each objective, she also developed a mastery checklist of actions that Gertrude would have to perform independently to show she had acquired the necessary know-how-to to proceed to ultimate play-worthy success. Winona's OT strategy was to break up each know-how transfer session into two 90-minute chunks per week during the next four weeks, planning each session based on Gertrude's progress. For the first four objectives, she decided to work with her cousin alone. However, since Mahj is played with four players, she planned to invite two of her friends to join them for practice games. Winona's long-term goal was to buy Gertrude a lovely Mah Jongg set for her birthday, which was five weeks after their first session.

Central to her strategy was an emphasis on transferring as much of her know-how to Gertrude as possible so that by the end of the five weeks, she would have enough Mah Jongg competency to participate in real play with other friends. The test checklists would play a major role in ensuring this happens.

Note that as soon as Winona laid out the know-how session objectives in verifiable terms, she created "tests" for Gertrude to demonstrate capability to perform along the way. These were not exams, but rather exercises and actions built into the transfer process. They were not scary or threatening—they naturally tied right into the learning activities.

In a sense, learning and playing is part strategy and part luck; because it's filled with a never-ending set of tests. Mastery requires continuous challenge and well-executed action to improve know-how and immediate application of acquired know-how-to to advance and succeed. OTs can be players who share their expertise and help others become better players—there is testing with feedback in every move. Fortunately, there are other methods of support as well. For example, you can find many books and online resources that can help a new Mah Jongg player. Winona wisely shared these resources with Gertrude, which further helped increase her confidence before joining the Mahj group.

Let's turn to a different situation, similar challenge, which we recently experienced. Imagine being asked to help five-year-old Seth discriminate between the lowercase alphabet letters "d" and "b." He was having difficulty with this at school, but our content know-how was certainly up to the task! However, we were less confident about our OT training capability with a frustrated, and by now anxious, five-year-old child.

CAN YOU TEST LITTLE CHILDREN?

We began by setting out a sequence of know-how transfer objectives for Seth to attain. For each objective, we created a test item to verify objective mastery. Then we created little stories and challenges to draw out the correct response for each test item and reinforce every success. We wanted him to experience the joy of successfully learning. We proceeded in this manner until he mastered each objective.

Let's see how this worked:

"Look at the duck (one of his favorite animals). See how his bum sticks out behind? 'd' is for duck and the round part of the 'd' also sticks out behind. Let's trace our finger over the 'd' on the duck's bum. Do it again and say 'd.' Where is the 'd' on the duck? Yes, and the round part is in the back! Trace it again with your finger. Yay for 'd'! And where is the round part of the letter? Yes, behind!"

Behind → d

"Now, let's look at the bear's belly. Is the bear's belly in the front of his body or behind? You're right. It's in front. The bear's belly is on the front of his body. Let's trace our finger over the 'b' on the bear. Do it again and say 'b.' And again. Yay for 'b' and 'belly!' Really good work!" (Seth gets a giggle out of saying belly.)

In front ← b

We showed the difference between the duck's bum sticking out behind (duck's bum = d) and the bear's belly sticking out in front (bear's belly = b), and then had Seth touch, trace, and practice.

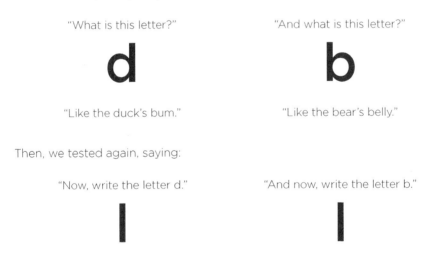

We kept testing with feedback, switching the "b" and "d" sides until he got it right every time.

"Wow! You're always right."

Finally, we tested once more, saying:

"Write the whole letter d
for the duck's bum."

"And write the whole letter b
for the bear's belly."

With each trial, we shared corrective feedback and guidance as necessary. We continuously confirmed and rewarded all successes, always making the activities fun! At the end, the big reward we gave Seth was two coloring books—one about ducks and one about bears. (Seth loves coloring!)

With two OTs and lots of testing, a joyful Seth got it. He loved the activities—and the coloring books.

Testing is a wonderful way to provide opportunities to achieve successful performance. Test frequently to monitor learning progress while letting the learner experience the wonderful sense of "I can do it!" Testing should not be a stress—instead it should be a delightful challenge and reinforcer. We close this chapter with a simple assertion: If the learners didn't learn (that is, they were not able to perform successfully), then the OT missed the boat. However, the contrary is also true: If learners were able to do it and the transfer of know-how to know-how-to demonstrably occurred, then, bravo!! Hats off to your magnificent success as an OT!

 REMEMBER
THIS

1. "The proof of the pudding is in the eating" means that (*successful training is demonstrated by the outcome/a know-how transfer transforms to novice know-how-to through careful planning*).

2. To ensure know-how has transferred to a new learner, you must (*always/never*) test.

3. To ensure that your tests are appropriate, you must first establish that they are (*rigorous/clear, meaningful, and logically sequenced*).

4. For learning purposes, the OT must set things up so that the learner (*is virtually guaranteed/feels somewhat uncertain*) of their successful performance.

5. Winona selected the objectives and tests for Gertrude to (*directly match the requirements of playing Mah Jongg/verify Gertrude could explain why she was doing something*).

6. The manner that the OT employs to test know-how transfer (*is/is not*) as important as the test itself.

7. We (*can/cannot*) accept that the OT was successful if the learner did not fully acquire the know-how-to.

Our choices and comments:

1. "The proof of the pudding is in the eating" means that *successful training is demonstrated by the outcome.*

2. To ensure know-how has transferred to a new learner, you *must always* test. Successful know-how transfer requires constant monitoring of learner performance with feedback and, as required, retesting.

3. To ensure that your tests are appropriate, you must first establish that they are *clear, meaningful, and logically sequenced.*

4. For learning purposes, the OT must set things up so that the learner *is virtually guaranteed* of their successful performance. A requirement of the OT is to do everything possible to drive learner performance outcome success.

5. Winona selected the objectives and tests for Gertrude to *directly match the requirements of playing Mah Jongg.*

6. The manner that the OT employs to test know-how transfer *is* as important as the test itself. The duck-bear example illustrates this. The manner we used to test Seth was carefully adapted to his age, uncertainties, and feedback needs.

7. We *cannot* accept that the OT was successful if the learner did not fully acquire the know-how-to. If the learner did not demonstrate correct behavior or outcome, then the OT was unsuccessful. Only demonstration of objective achievement is the proof of the pudding.

In know-how transfer, the learner must be able to do it. You'll know that the know-how transfer was a smashing success if they:

- arrived at the intended destination
- used self-checkout for a cart full of groceries
- produced a perfectly shaped table leg using an electronic lathe
- parked the car without incident in the designated spot
- filled the bucket with milk from the cow's udder without spilling a drop.

Hail the conquering OT as hero and show their brilliant use of tests as proof!

What More Do I Need to Do?

Congratulations! As a full-fledged OT, you are almost there. This book has packed into it just about everything we believe is useful for transferring your know-how to others who do not yet possess your capability to perform. This chapter provides a few more bits of advice to polish your OT skills as you head off to train, teach, coach, mentor, or engage in any activity that results in another person being able to do what you can.

The Three Cs

We begin at a high level with some powerful advice that we received from a great trainer-educator many years ago. Dugan Laird has since passed away, but his words remain deeply embedded within us. The advice came in the form of a lesson entitled the Three Cs of a Great Trainer: Competence, Confidence, and Caring.

Competence

This is the ability of the trainer to impart knowledge in ways that everyone involved will value. Competence, in this context, does not just refer to the trainer's subject matter know-how. Of course, it's necessary to make sure that the content taught is accurate and applicable and contains the most appropriate material, the right examples, and the OT's own knowledge and insights.

However, in our OT context, competence mostly refers to how well you perform as a true trainer. This includes putting the principles, models, tools, and guidance in this book into practice. It also means conscientiously applying what you have learned and critically monitoring yourself in the OT role. Competence means doing the right things and doing them correctly. The proof of your competence resides in the successful outcome of your learners.

Confidence

Your own self-assurance as you train—even in simply helping someone learn how to play a new game—can be defined as confidence. How you communicate, the tone you use, your smile, a relaxed demeanor, and the sure way you guide your learner all convey confidence, along with the message that they will succeed.

Caring

The third C centers on the OT's sincere desire for learner success. This is shown in the communication of positive, supportive emotion. We hope that you sense how deeply we care that you perform well in your training role. Caring requires the OT to demonstrate to each learner, not just by word, but by tone, gesture, and deed how much they wish for them to demonstrate that they can do it. As you transfer your know-how into their know-how-to, your caring radiates encouragement and provides inspiration, stimulating their efforts and accomplishments.

Are you manifesting the three Cs in the transfer process? Use this self-assessment to find out.

Self-Assessment: The Fourth Wall

We call it the fourth wall because it begins with this assertion: Training is not transmission; rather, it is transformation. Almost anyone can transmit subject matter content if they have the know-how—list standard operating procedures or describe the steps in a pre-inspection audit of a potential fire-hazard site. It's much harder, however, to effectively transform learners into capable know-how-to performers. This section affirms that your success as an OT in any context depends on your answering "yes" to each of these questions:

- ❑ Am I excited about helping my learners learn and perform?
- ❑ Do I deeply care about what I say to my learners and how I say it?
- ❑ Am I there at all times for my learners?
- ❑ Do I care that my learners master the challenge and succeed in the outcome?
- ❑ Do I believe that, as an OT, my job is to serve my learners?

As you can see, these questions are closely linked to the three Cs. They emphasize the sense of confidence to serve one's learners, desire and ability to do well by them, and care about their success.

Training in the form of effective knowledge and skill transfer succeeds when communication between any trainer, including you as an OT, and learner is open and free. A critical role of the trainer is to remove all obstacles to communication.

Let's visualize the training-learning setting as a theater, with the OT as the actor and the learners as the audience. The stage has four walls: the backstage wall, the left and right wings, and, most important of all, the fourth, seemingly invisible wall, between the actor and the audience (the trainer and the learners). Pretend that the fourth wall is built of impenetrable bricks, each one an obstacle to communication:

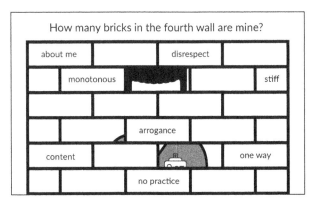

Your job as the OT is to eliminate any obstacles you create that inhibit communication. As you work at this, continually ask yourself, "How many bricks in this fourth wall are mine?" Work brick by brick to pry each one loose and discard it. Watch as the wall begins to crumble until none are left and communication flows freely.

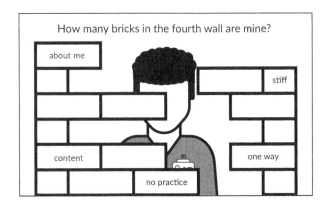

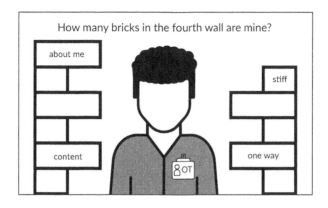

The result is open communication and a complete transfer of know-how.

Use It or Lose It

This cliché rings true. We have used the term *automaticity* before, whereby deliberate and focused practice results in non-thinking, unconscious, fluent performance in applying new know-how-to. Provide lots of practice with feedback until the learner can do it automatically. This is key for long-term storage and retrieval. Don't believe us? Have you ever taken a foreign language class and then not used that language for even a short length of time? The result? Words, expressions, and grammar all evaporate. Generate opportunities for practice and offer recommendations for continued use to extend and strengthen learning and performance. In the meantime, apply this principle to yourself as an OT. Keep rehearsing your know-how transfer skills and constantly monitor how well you perform. This will result in your own unconscious competence as an OT.

Anything I Can Do You Can Do Better

We have emphasized the importance of building confidence. Consider creating mini challenges as you train that let the learner surpass you. These challenges will drive the learner's motivation to constantly improve or perform with more self-assurance. Develop increasingly more difficult learning-scenario challenges to demonstrate how, once the learner has got it and can do it, they can compete with and even outperform the OT. However, make sure it's done in a non-threatening way that's fun and playful challenge. Here are a few examples:

- **Hockey training.** Start with the basics of a slapshot. Increase the difficulty of the angle. Place obstacles between the puck and the goal. As difficulty levels increase, compete with the novice, at first handicapping yourself severely then reducing your handicaps as their performance improves. Continue to encourage your learner to outperform you and build in opportunities for success.

- **Navigating an obstacle course.** As above, add to the difficulty level as your learner's performance capability grows. Then, inject elements of competition by adding you or more advanced competitors until your learner can beat everyone. (With young children, this may have to be contrived; for example, "You must answer five multiplication table flash cards in three minutes or less. I must complete ten in the same time period. Let's see who can finish first!")

- **Searching databases.** Practice data retrieval with increasingly more complex scenarios, shorter time limits, and greater error consequence.

- **Playing chess.** Select increasingly higher-performing opponents, decrease the time allotment for moves, and try to solve harder chess problems. In all cases, make sure the challenges you design are attainable.

- **In the workplace.** Try upping the responsibilities of a worker or the difficulty or precision level required of them.

This creates a win-win situation for everyone. The learner gets to practice more, improves capability, builds automaticity (hence retention), strengthens competency, and increases confidence. However, as the learner builds capability, the OT should remember to monitor for learner overconfidence.

As a final note, you base your success on your learners' independent performance—the right set of actions resulting in valued accomplishment away from the OT. When this is attained, you have not only met this book's goals but also your own. Your learners have taken full ownership of your know-how—as they should!

 REMEMBER THIS

You know what to do with the following statements. Go for it!

1. The three Cs of training refer to (*cooperation, communication, and capability/competence, confidence, and caring*).

2. Within the context of this chapter, competence (*refers/does not just refer*) to subject matter know-how.

3. The fourth wall is the (*clearly visible brick/invisible*) barrier between the OT and the learner in the know-how transfer process.

4. "Use it or lose it" refers to the (*learner's/learner and the OT's*) need to maintain and improve their ability to apply acquired know-how-to in the real world.

5. Practice that includes placing novice learners into competitive situations (*should never/can be*) used to stimulate performance improvement.

6. Learners should (*ultimately/never*) assume ownership of newly acquired and mastered know-how-to.

And as we see it…

1. The three Cs of training refer to *competence, confidence, and caring.*
2. Within the context of this chapter, competence *does not just refer* to subject matter know-how. It also refers to the OT's capability to successfully transfer subject matter know-how.
3. The fourth wall is the *invisible* barrier between the OT and the learner in the know-how transfer process.
4. "Use it or lose it" refers to the *learner and the OT's need to* maintain and improve their ability to apply acquired know-how-to in the real world.
5. Practice that includes placing novice learners into competitive situations *can be used* to stimulate performance improvement.
6. Learners should *ultimately* assume ownership of newly acquired and mastered know-how-to.

Congratulations! You have almost arrived at the end of *Know-How.* We have one final chapter on where you go from here. As we have often mentioned, it is not best practice to simply wave goodbye to the person with whom you have worked without giving them ways to deal with the unanticipated challenges of the world. Whenever possible, provide a means for reinforcing, upgrading, and enhancing their know-how-to so they can improve and grow in their capability. Turn to chapter 12 to learn what's still ahead for you.

12

I'm Convinced!
How Do I Learn More?

The effectiveness of an OT is continuously evolving. To this point, we have provided a foundation for transforming your know-how into others' know-how-to. Now you might be wondering, what are the immediate and long-term follow-up steps for continued growth? This final chapter presents recommendations for enhancing your OT performance.

Practice! Practice! Practice!

This is the basic rule for anything you want to improve yourself in. Just as you tell your learner, proficiency comes with deliberate practice. So, practice. Fine tune. Then practice the refinement. Take every opportunity to hone your ability to:

- Really hear what the person who turns to or is assigned to you for help wishes to achieve. What is the desired outcome? Listen, repeat back, and clarify what your mission is. Work hard on the diagnosis and the goal. This may be the hardest part of your task. If you correctly determine what is needed, the rest of the effort will be much easier.
- Observe carefully everything your novice learner does. Gauge their entry level skills, prior knowledge, confidence, and characteristics to determine how best to interact with them to build the most appropriate form of communication.
- As you engage, watch the learner's reactions to what you say and do. Practice different ways of interacting with a novice learner.
- Try out different know-how transfer methods. Gather feedback and try again.
- Each opportunity to assist is a practice session. Seize every one of them to learn from.

Be a Learner

Put yourself into situations where you can acquire know-how-to capability from others. Ask a friend or colleague to teach you how to execute a task. Ask your child or a neighbor's kid to show you how to use an app or play a game. Listen, engage, and try it out. Observe yourself and your trainer. Note what you're going through as well as what works and what doesn't.

Then record how you feel and analyze what went well and what did not work for you.

From Our Journal

When we purchased a new, high-end dishwasher, we found, after running a few loads, that our dishes, glassware, and utensils were not looking as sparkling clean as we had hoped. We first discussed the matter with our salesperson, who encouraged us to try a different dishwasher detergent. Still unhappy with the result, we scheduled a visit with a certified repair person recommended by the manufacturer.

The dishwasher expert arrived and soon began lecturing us at length on how we had been loading our dishes improperly. We asked him to share his know-how with us so we could improve. He launched into a demonstration and took over completely. Being rather large, he also blocked our view of what was going on. We interrupted him politely and explained that we were writing a book on sharing know-how and that this was a great example case. We asked him to start again, this time allowing us to guide his know-how transfer session to help him help us "get it better." We would also demonstrate back to him as we learned.

The inducement of a strong cup of coffee and freshly baked cookies softened him up to go another round. The second time through we got him to ask us what we wanted to accomplish and made him repeat what we had said. As we guided him in training us, he got into the swing of things. By the end, we insisted that he scrutinize us loading the dishwasher (a test). He corrected some of our errors (for example, fork tines up; dessert cups in the lower rack, tall items away from the spinning water distributer).

His attitude when working with customers, he admitted, was usually one of, "I've been doing this for 30 years. Listen. Watch. Learn. This saves me time and you, money." He thanked us for making him listen to us. And shared that he had learned a lot.

His final words to us were: "Maybe I'll listen more and talk less. I like that piece about having the customer demo for me. Cute trick!"

And we learned a lot as learners too.

Teach a Young Person How to Do Something

Train your teenager to drive a car or your child to mow the lawn. Monitor your and your learner's emotions as well as your behaviors. Spend time as a volunteer in a daycare center and teach children how to dress a mannequin, set the table, or tie their shoelaces. These are amazing challenges. Be helpful and watch how these little ones can help you grow your OT skills.

Train or Be Trained by Someone Close

Have your significant other train you to cook a meal or set the table. Train them to measure ingredients, mix a drink, or taste wine. Use these intimate and informal trials to observe and rate your emotions and nonverbal signals during the interactions. Raise your awareness about what goes on within the learner beyond the words and gestures that occur during the training-learning interplay.

Eavesdrop

Listen and observe when others are teaching someone how to do something, explaining a new and unfamiliar task, or simply giving directions on how to find a location. Note their words, tone, and the learner's reactions. What did they do that was good? Unproductive? Off-putting? Reinforcing? Confusing?

Observe Others Doing Formal Training

Ask to sit in on a training class to see how a full-time professional does it. What can you take away to improve your competencies? What do you notice that you should avoid? If possible, debrief with the trainer or students. Ask what helped them learn the most during the class. And what helped the least.

Train Others to Become OTs

One of the best ways to learn is by teaching. This forces you to think through what you must do, practice, and rehearse. It also helps you focus on your skills and techniques and allows you to observe the results of your efforts through others. The more you train others to become effective OTs, the better the OT you will become. Always debrief your sessions.

Request feedback using specific, prepared questions as well as spontaneous, open-ended ones.

Frequently Debrief Your Learners

You have trained them. Now, step back and interview your learners (or ask others to do this) to obtain useful, usable feedback on how you performed. In the most non-threatening manner possible, probe them to draw out what worked, what didn't, what was confusing, and what might have helped make the training better.

We could have added a lot more to our list, but instead we'll add just one more suggestion: **read.** There are a lot of books and articles out there about training. There are also many courses on how to effectively teach, train, and communicate. There are also organizations that can help you further your knowledge about the incredible world of helping others develop their capabilities. Within this realm lie astonishingly wonderful career paths to explore.

Whether you're a manager, specialist, counselor, tutor, advisor, fellow worker, parent, helpful person, coach, teammate, big brother or sister, or occasional trainer, this book was written for you!

Learn More

Contact us to share thoughts, ask questions, or simply chat. You can reach us at hstolovitch@gmail.com or ekeeps@gmail.com. If you have any interest in reading more of our books, here are few:

Telling Ain't Training

Beyond Telling Ain't Training Fieldbook

Training Ain't Performance

Beyond Training Ain't Performance Fieldbook

For more about training, learning, and talent development and careers in these fields, contact the Association for Talent Development, which also publishes many books, reports, magazines, and other related materials. ATD also offers numerous workshops, conferences, and other events.

Notes

1. Training, "2018 Training Industry Report," *Training* 55(6): 18–31. trainingmag.com/sites/default/files/trn-2018-industry-report.pdf.
2. The most authoritative compendium of research on expertise is *The Cambridge Handbook of Expertise and Expert Performance*. This large volume deals with many aspects of expertise across a broad variety of domains. The two characteristics of expertise cited here are related to the very nature of the subject: expertise is the ability to perform in unique and extraordinary ways but not necessarily able to explain how they perform so well; Experts and novices in a given area think and process information about their subject matter very differently. The greater the expertise, the greater the gap between expert and novice. K. Anders Ericsson, Neil Charness, Paul J. Feltovich, and Robert R. Hoffman, *The Cambridge Handbook of Expertise and Expert Performance* (Cambridge: Cambridge University Press, 2006).
3. Harold D. Stolovitch, *Design, Development and Evaluation of "High Seas"—A Training Vehicle for Proficiency Maintenance of Collision Regulations,* Final Report to the Canadian Navy (Montreal, PQ: HSA Ltd, 1987); Harold D. Stolovitch, Erica J. Keeps, and Cdr. R.H. Kerr, "High Seas: A Performance Maintenance Game," paper presented at the 27th annual conference of the National Society for Performance & Instruction, Denver, Colorado, March 1989 (Encore Track). For a full version of the paper, visit hpttreasures.files .wordpress.com/2020/01/high-seas-a-performance-maintenance-game.pdf
4. For more detail, please see *Telling Ain't Training,* 2nd ed. In this book, the model has been somewhat adapted to even the simplest of know-how

transfer examples. The model, principles, and applications can be scaled to any level of complexity. Stolovitch and Keeps, *Telling Ain't Training*, 2nd ed. (Alexandria VA: ATD Press, 2011).

5. The earliest published reference we could find of "sage on the stage" is in the article "'Gifted Students' Classes Offered," which quotes Alice Johnson, secondary education supervisor of Kentucky's Greenup County School District using the phrase: "Mrs. Johnson said the teacher for the gifted and talented will be more of a 'guide on the side' rather than a 'sage on the stage.' In other words, she explained, 'each student will have a lot of freedom to pursue their special field of interest." From the August 6, 1981, of *Harlan Daily Express*. See also Alison King, "From Sage on the Stage to Guide on the Side," *College Teaching* 41, no. 1 (1993): 30-35.

6. A good article that describes the negative effects of stress on memory is Susanne Vogle and Lars Schwabe, "Memory Under Stress: Implications for the Classroom," *NPJ Science of Learning* 1, no. 16011 (2016). nature.com/articles /npjscilearn201611.

7. Anna Mulrine, "No Prank: On Halloween, US Military Forces Train for Zombie Apocalypse," Christian Science Monitor, October 31, 2012. csmonitor.com/USA/Military/2012/1031/No-prank-On-Halloween-US -military-forces-train-for-zombie-apocalypse.

8. Harold and Erica have created knowledge transfer games for the Canadian Navy and other military groups. "Northern Adventures" guides individual officer decision-making under continuously changing, hazardous conditions, while "High Seas" deals with the application of collision avoidance regulations while in command of a naval vessel.

9. Numerous studies show how little training gets successfully transferred to the world beyond where the training occurred. One of the main causes is lack of follow-up support by trainers, management, peers, and other resources. See, for example, Rebecca Grossman and Eduardo Salas, "The Transfer of Training: What Really Matters," *International Journal of Training & Development* 15, no. 2 (2011): 103–120.

10. The earliest appearance of the proverb "The proof of the pudding is in the eating" is in William Camden's *Remaines of a Greater Worke Concerning Britaine, 1605*. In ancient times a pudding was savory sausage mixture, but more recently it's become popularized as a sweet or savory dessert.

About the Authors

Known as "the Ain't book series authors," **Harold D. Stolovitch**, CPT, and **Erica J. Keeps**, CPT, co-wrote *Telling Ain't Training, Training Ain't Performance*, and their companion field guides. They were also co-editors for the first two editions of the *Handbook of Performance Technology*, the major reference work in the field. Together they have devoted 90-plus years to making workplace learning more effective and enjoyable.

As the principals of HSA Learning & Performance Solutions, they specialize in the design and development of learning and human performance systems across a wide range of organizations, such as GM, Chrysler, Toyota, BOMI (Building Owners and Managers Institute International), Bank of Montreal, Prudential, Hewlett-Packard, Canadian Pacific Railway, CDW, the Canadian Navy, the USDA, WW (Weight Watchers International), Century 21, Cisco Systems, AT&T, Forcepoint, Chevron, and Sanofi Pasteur, as well as the military and health and governmental agencies. They also conduct workshops internationally on training delivery, instructional design, and performance consulting.

Harold holds a bachelor's degree and certificate of graduate studies from McGill University in Canada, and a PhD in instructional systems technology from Indiana University. He has conducted extensive research in the field, developed countless instructional materials, and authored more than 300 articles, reports, book chapters, and books. Harold has won numerous awards and is a professor emeritus with the Université de Montréal.

Erica holds a bachelor's degree from the University of Michigan and a master's degree in educational psychology from Wayne State University. Her career has included senior-level learning and performance positions with a variety of organizations. She has produced and managed the production of hundreds of instructional materials and performance management systems. Erica has also published extensively in the fields of workplace learning and performance.

This husband and wife team of nearly 40 years currently resides in Los Angeles, California, with their canine companion, Buttercup.